CRY

OF THE

INNOCENTS

ABORTION AND THE RACE TOWARDS JUDGMENT

CRY

OF THE

INNOCENTS

ABORTION AND THE RACE TOWARDS JUDGMENT

JOHN O. ANDERSON

With Doug Brendel

Bridge Publishing, Inc.
South Plainfield, NJ

Cry of the Innocents
© John O. Anderson 1984
All rights reserved
Printed in the United States of America
ISBN: 0-88270-586-5
Library of Congress catalog number: 85-070539
Bridge Publishing, Inc.
2500 Hamilton Blvd.
South Plainfield, NJ 07080

DEDICATION

To my wife Esther
and our children
Cathi,
Timothy,
Douglas
and Robin.

We rejoice in LIFE.

v

CONTENTS

ACKNOWLEDGEMENTS

I am deeply indebted to many people who have helped on this project. In addition to Doug Brendel, who labored with me in the writing, I would like to acknowledge the work of Steve Clark, an excellent writer who took my research and helped birth the first draft.

Another person I need to recognize is Dr. Murray Norris. He was the one who first urged me to write *The Cry of the Innocents* message, after he heard it on a cassette tape.

I must also express the very deepest thanks to my own beautiful church fellowship which I am privileged to serve as pastor. How they have supported me, giving me the freedom to write and the means to travel both in America and overseas! I am humbled at all they have done.

And then there is my beautiful wife, Esther, whose counsel and encouragement throughout this project have been immeasurable. How I thank God for her.

Everyone who has helped in this book has done so with one motivation: to speak up for those who cannot speak for themselves.

FUNERAL TRAIN

Where are the children, and mothers? . . .
I shudder from the news.
My God! We're killing thousands,
    without blinking an eye.
My God! We're killing thousands, believing lies.

Have we lost now?
Our country's dying now.
Does it matter to you now?
We aren't free now.
People dying in the streets now.
Doesn't it matter to you now?

Have we been blind too long?
And forgotten Who put us together?
Is it in God we trust?

She's young and lonely, but she's made a mistake.
And there's so much out there for her future,
So why should she wait nine months or so,
Just to pay for her mistake?
And so we take it away!

—Anne Herring, "Killing Thousands"
© 1981, Latter Rain Music

The train rattled along the tracks, and I jostled slightly in my seat as it went. My father had died, and I was returning to my home in Oregon after the funeral in California.

My schedule as a pastor in Klamath Falls was continuously hectic, and the trip was a welcome break. Taking the train gave me a few extra hours of solitude, for relaxation, for study. And I needed time to absorb the reality of my dad's death.

I had brought along a book to read—a Bible commentary, not exactly your popular paperback variety of book, but something I was very much looking forward to. It was something relatively new by Francis L. Anderson and David Noel Freedman, one of Doubleday's Anchor Bible Series of commentaries, on the prophetic book of Hosea. Perhaps any other passenger on that train would have found the book intimidating or ponderous, and even I expected it to be simply another rather standard investigation of Scripture passages that I had already studied many times.

But that trip, and that book, changed my life.

By the time I got off the train in Klamath Falls, I had wept deeply inside and prayed. I had been shocked and scorched in my spirit; my intellect had been confronted and challenged as never before.

And that train ride was not the end of it, but rather a beginning. As the engine slowed and the brakes hissed, I was only beginning a journey that would take me through the Word of God again and again, and through a hundred other books and commentaries, and finally into my own church pulpit, and onto public platforms from Klamath Falls to Rome, until I had been completely consumed by the strange and disturbing revelation that God began to give me on that train ride.

The journey began with Hosea, a bizarre character by modern standards, so intent on doing what God told him that he married a prostitute in obedience to the Lord— simply for the sake of the act's symbolism!

It was the eighth century before Christ, a pivotal time for both of the twin kingdoms of Israel and Judah. Both nations were at their zeniths in political influence and economic security. Jeroboam II and Uzziah, kings over the north and south, had defeated their enemies on a grand scale, expanding their borders and influencing civilization far beyond their national boundaries. The people realized they had entered upon an era of unsurpassed well-being. They believed their wealth and good fortune were God's reward for their supposed faithfulness to Him.

But all was not as it seemed. The second half of that marvelous eighth century B.C. brought that bright age to a disastrous end—and the tragic decay of a nation began.

This is where Hosea's strange, profound ministry comes on the scene. His recorded work began during the latter years of the reign of Jeroboam II—a man responsible for a number of crimes against God and His people. As I read the commentary on Hosea, I read of Jeroboam's flagrant violations of his nation's sacred covenant with God. In fact, Jeroboam's administration presided over such gross sins that it took *two* prophets, Amos and Hosea, to address them all! Amos looked at "the gap between the covenant requirements in the social and economic spheres and the realities in the kingdom of Israel," while Hosea spoke "even more vehemently about religious commitments and cult practices, charging the establishment with nothing less than idolatry, apostasy, and cultic enormities, including sexual promiscuity and human sacrifice."[1]

The prophecies of Hosea and Amos pointed to the eventual downfall of Israel. Israel fell captive to the Assyrians in 722 B.C., and Judah fell captive to the Babylonians less than 150 years later.

Essentially, Hosea was an "end-times" prophet of his day. We have many of those types in today's world too. Unfortunately, most of them seem to be preoccupied with the *schedule* of the end-times, rather than the *message* of the end-times.

Unlike our contemporary end-times expositors, Hosea was more concerned with the message of God for His people as they faced their "last days," rather than the schedule of events. He wasn't concerned with *when* the demise of Israel would occur. Hosea was concerned with *why* the people were subject to God's coming judgment, and *how* they could avoid spiritual disaster and find redemption. Hosea's concern was the salvation of God's people—turning them back to Him.

As the train rumbled along, I realized that there were even more similarities between Hosea's time and our own. And those similarities intrigued me. I wondered what exactly the elements were that led to Israel's downfall.

And then, a phrase from Hosea 4:2 jumped from the page, and began resounding through my mind: "they break all bounds . . . bloodshed follows bloodshed."

Murder begets murder. Murder of innocent life begets more murder of innocent life.

As this recurring phrase played in my mind, bits and pieces of recent news articles and magazine stories and other sources flashed in counterpoint.

A quote by Albert Schweitzer surfaced: "If a man loses reverence for any part of life, he will lose his reverence for all of life."

As all of these thoughts began to congeal, an awful

4

realization began to dawn: Israel's judgment and downfall came because of their ultimate sin—the killing of innocent victims by official sanction. They "shed innocent blood," according to Psalm 106:38, "even the blood of their sons and of their daughters, whom they sacrificed unto the idols of Canaan: and the land was polluted with blood."

And because of this "was the wrath of the Lord kindled against his people insomuch that he abhorred his own inheritance" (Ps. 106:40).

But it was a single striking paragraph in the commentary on Hosea that would deeply sober me:

> Idolatrous and apostate worship has two outstanding features, on both of which the prophet pours out his vehemence. Sexual promiscuity in the fertility cult undermines the moral structure of the covenant and is a gross violation of the basic requirements on community life under God. Furthermore, it leads in some circuitous way to the *culminating sin against God and people*, that is, the *shedding of innocent blood*. This is not ordinary murder, itself an ultimate crime, but *officially sanctioned human sacrifice.*[2]

When I read those words again, I stopped reading and put the book down. One word came flooding into my mind: *Abortion!*

And I saw that the issue of abortion biblically is *the shedding of innocent blood!*

No, brutal child sacrifice does not exist today as it did in Israel's day. But abortion is its ghastly counterpart. Today, millions of innocent babies are sacrificed—by official sanction. It is done in the name of secular humanism's *causes célèbre:* "the right of a woman to her own body," "every child should be wanted," "the viability of the fetus," or "the right to choose."

In fact, we are slaughtering the most innocent of the innocents: unborn babies. And it is done through the decree of law, having been legalized by the Supreme Court in the famous *Roe v. Wade* decision of 1973.

I looked out the window of the train.

In later research, I would read a searing statement by James Dobson that would stir me again: "I see abortion as the most significant moral issue of our time. In fact, I feel that the ministers of this country (of the world) are someday going to have to answer for their unwillingness to confront this issue head-on. It cannot be right to take an *innocent little child* whom God is forming in his mother's womb, and leave him to die on a porcelain table."[3]

Suddenly, as I sat in that rumbling train car, I realized that the issue was more than a passing social concern. It was murder—but worse, murder of innocents, the shedding of innocent blood. And, by the standard God had set for His people, most terrible of all—the shedding of innocent blood by official sanction.

Legalized abortion suddenly seemed to line up precisely alongside Israel's ritualized child sacrifices in several frightening ways. And even as their incredible violation of God's covenant sowed the seeds of their own destruction, so I saw, in my mind's eye, America, and a world, racing toward its own doom, "playing with a loaded gun."

Israel's acts had been called "the culminating sin against God." Now I saw America reaching that same outer limit.

And the only possible outcome: catastrophe.

Notes for Chapter One

[1] Anderson & Freedman, *Hosea,* Doubleday, 1980, p. 38.
[2] Ibid., p. 49.
[3] James Dobson, "Theism and the Modern Mind," *Christianity Today,* May 7, 1982.

CHILD SACRIFICE

First Moloch, horrid King besmear'd with blood
Of human sacrifice, and parents' tears,
Though for the noise of Drums and Timbrels loud
Their children's cries unheard, that passed through fire
To his grim Idol.

—John Milton
Paradise Lost

And sullen Moloch, fled,
Hath left in shadows dread
    His burning idol all of blackest hue;
In vain with Cymbal's ring
They call the grisly king,
    In dismal dance about the furnace blue;
The brutish gods of Nile as fast,
Isis and Orus, and the Dog Anubis haste.
    —John Milton
    On the Morning of Christ's Nativity

It was the night of sacrifice. The air was heavy and damp with sticky summer heat. Sweat covered one's body like an oily film.

9

Molech's image glowed against the dark, deeply clouded sky. The figure was ominous, awesome. A beautifully sculpted, dramatic bull's head atop a powerful, muscled body of a man. Tilka's heart pounded in anticipation of the night's sacrifice. It was anticipation, bred of devotion, yet mixed with anguish and silent terror. It was her firstborn son that was to die in Molech's glowing, red-hot arms.

Tilka knew there was no alternative but to sacrifice her tiny son. It was the law, and it was the way of her people. All her life, she had worshiped before Molech and Baal and the other gods and goddesses. When she had come of age, her family went to the temple together, each going in to the temple prostitutes. That is where she lost her virginity, in the service of their gods. She knew it was the right thing to do.

And she had taken part in the sacrifices, watching other mothers place their innocent newborn sons in the out-stretched arms of the terrible, flame-filled Molech. It was a humbling experience. She always felt sympathy and pride for the mothers who gave up their children. It was necessary to insure good harvests and even future fertility in the women.

Tilka knew that one day she would have the opportunity to serve the gods with the ultimate sacrifice. She knew she would have to give up her firstborn son, and she knew she would. It had to be done. It was the law, and it was the way of her people. She was always proud to be a servant of Baal and El and Molech.

She dressed in her most elegant and revealing gown. Tonight she would not only offer her son to Molech, but she would again offer her body to the temple prostitutes as usual at the height of the worship ceremony. As she prepared herself, she did her best to steel her thoughts against the pain of losing her child. She had to be perfectly numb and emotionless as her innocent infant son was rolled into the hungry flames—the ever ravenous flames. If she cried or gave any indication of sorrow, the sacrifice of her son would be meaningless, and she and her husband would be barred from the temple.

Tilka went over to where her son was sleeping. He had just nursed and was sleeping soundly. She wanted him to remain as quiet and peaceful as possible as he faced the ordeal. He was such a beautiful baby boy, with handsome features and a surprisingly full head of hair. He was flawless. As she wrapped him in his blanket, momentary regret and pain flashed through her breaking heart. Yet she didn't dare question the gods' motives, not even to herself.

As Tilka and her husband approached the hill of sacrifice, the sounds of the ceremony drifted toward them. Loud drums were being beaten rhythmically, and other instruments added to the deep din. In the distance, to the west across the mountains, thunder rumbled in counterpoint, and intermittent heat lightning flashed eerily. It was a perfect night for sacrifice, for the gods were joining the worship.

Tilka shivered in the chilly air, yet she was covered with a cold, slimy sweat. She and her husband walked into the circle of worshipers, and carried their son to the priests. As they moved nearer the blazing Molech, the music became louder and more frenzied. For a moment, Tilka wanted to scream and run, taking her child with her. Yet, from deeper inside, she knew the sacrifice was right and good. And she knew she would obey her gods as she had done all her life.

She placed her son in the priest's arms. The priest lifted the child toward the image and began chanting to the great god Molech. Attendants threw more wood into the furnace, making the fire roar with new intensity.

The music was raucous, a frantic din. It always got loudest during a sacrifice—perhaps, Tilka guessed, to drown out the cries of the dying infant as it screamed in agony and pain. The temple prostitutes, both male and female, scantily clad, began to dance sensuously before the image of Molech, enticing the god to observe their ceremony and take heed of the sacrifice.

Tilka stood frozen, emotionless as she watched the priests handle her son. Each one took the child and intoned over it, praying to Molech, blessing the sacrifice. Finally the child was handed to the high priest who stood before Molech's outstretched arms. Tilka had never noticed until tonight how frightening and evil Molech's image appeared.

The music reached a deafening peak. The dancers twirled in obscene frenzy, other worshipers joining them. It was as if a mass hysteria had begun to creep over the congregation of devout worshipers.

The priest slowly lifted the child skyward as he woke and began crying innocently for his mother. But his mother stood still. Suddenly, the priest, not able to get too near the glowing, intensely hot image of Molech, threw the crying child into the god's outstretched arms. The innocent child screamed in terror and pain. The odor of charred flesh immediately filled the air with its awful stench. For several moments, the child's frantic death cries could be dimly heard beneath the noise of the instruments. The priest took a rod and pushed the blackened, charred body deeper into the flames, and the crying stopped.

The baby was finally dead. Molech was served.

The ceremony had now reached a fevered pitch. Tilka, feeling as if she had turned to stone inside, approached one of the male prostitutes, and they disappeared into the temple. The rest of the night, she buried the last traces of emotion beneath a torrent of sexual activity and drunkenness. She and her husband were well respected by the community, and devout followers of the gods. They would be honored for several days because of the sacrifice of their son. By the standards and laws of their land, they had done the right thing.

Twenty-eight centuries later, Mary moved about the bedroom slowly, gathering her belongings into a small suitcase. Today was the day she would go to the hospital. The hot summer sun glared brightly through the window. Mary was hot and sweating in spite of the air conditioning.

Mary was three months pregnant. But she and her husband had both decided that they didn't want the child. They both had successful careers, and they had only been married three yars. Her husband, John, felt it was too early for a child. A child, he had said, would be an intrusion on their time together. She had agreed, even though they spent very little time alone with each other. They were both very involved in their careers.

Also, Mary wanted the abortion for another reason. She wasn't really sure if the child was her husband's or her lover's. She had been seeing Allen for slightly more than three months.

Allen wasn't Mary's first lover, either. There had been one other since she married John, and several before her marriage. In fact, even John had been one of her pre-marital affairs. Mary was a modern, liberated, free-spirited woman.

She lost her virginity in high school. Her mother knew about it, and had even given her the Pill. Mary was also aware of her parents' sexual activity outside of their marriage. It was the socially accepted thing to be promiscuous. It had not even been much of a shock to learn that her husband John was having an affair with one of their old college pals, Elizabeth. Elizabeth was Mary' former roommate, and one of her best friends.

Mary had often discussed abortion with her friends. I was a common topic. Several in her social circle were actively involved in lobbying for pro-abortion laws, and many had had abortions. All for very selfish reasons, Mary conceded, but—she felt—justifiable reasons. And Mary had figured all along she would probably have to face th decision to abort one day. After all, she reasoned, no birth control method is one hundred percent effective. It was perhaps just a matter of time.

Mary finished packing and carried her bag into the living room. She had to spend at least one night in the hospital in case of complications. The doctor had explained there wasn't anything to really worry about, but Mary agreed with him that it was probably the best thing to do. Besides, she wanted to be away from John, alone, so she could think. She knew she was doing the right thing; all her friends had told her so. But, even so, she had some reservations. The doctor' descriptions of the various methods of abortion had disturbed her.

The first method he had discussed with her was "D and C," the common abbreviation for "dilation and curettage." This procedure, he explained, is usually done before the twelfth or thirteenth week of pregnancy. It involves stretching the cervix to allow for a curette— tiny hoe-shaped instrument—to be inserted. Then, the walls of the uterus are scraped, and the baby's body is also cut into pieces—and, with the placenta, is pulled out of the womb.

14

As an alternative, the doctor went on to describe suction abortion. This method is similar to the D and C, except that instead of the curette, a powerful suction tube is inserted into the uterus. The suction tears the body of the baby into pieces, and sucks the pieces with the placenta into a jar. More than two thirds of abortions are done by suction.

A third option available to Mary was the saline abortion. A long needle is inserted through the mother's abdomen and directly into the sac containing the amniotic fluid surrounding the baby. A solution of concentrated salt is then injected into the sac. The saline solution is absorbed by the baby into its lungs and gastrointestinal tract, producing a change in the osmotic pressure in his tiny body. The outer layer of skin is also burned off due to the high concentration of salt. Normally, the mother then goes into labor and hours later delivers a dead, shriveled baby.

But what disturbed Mary more than the doctor's graphic descriptions of abortion methods was the fact that there was still the possibility of a live birth. She worried that after all the trouble to get an abortion, she and John might be stuck with parenthood after all.

In spite of these fears, she knew there was no alternative. John drove her to the hospital. They both were silent, not knowing what to say to one another. Besides, they had already talked it out between themselves, and with their friends. They knew they were doing the right thing. They really weren't ready for children, and it would be senseless to have an unwanted child around.

Mary shivered in spite of the day's warmth. She and John walked into the hospital and down the long corridors to her room. Others awaiting abortion were also housed on Mary's floor. Ironically, they had to go through the pediatric and maternity wards to reach her room. Seeing the younger children in pediatrics and the pink, newborn babies in maternity had touched something inside Mary. For a moment she felt panic, and she wanted to run away somewhere . . . where she could have her child and see him grow. But the panic subsided as she rationalized these silly urges away.

Later that evening, after John had gone, the doctor came in. Since Mary was so far along in her pregnancy, they had decided on a saline abortion. Mary felt it was the least violent, least brutal way to dispose of the unwanted fetus inside her.

Mary had taken great care to adopt a very rational, non-feeling air concerning what was happening to her. By careful practice she had begun to think of the baby growing inside as an "it." The doctors had even referred to what remained after an abortion as the "product" of an abortion. She decided that it was not much different than having a tumor removed. It wasn't a tiny human being inside her, it was merely an unwanted piece of tissue—a "product of conception," or "POC," a nurse had called it. However, Mary wondered, if it survived abortion attempts, what would "it" be then?

It has to be killed in the womb, she thought, it can't get out. To try to kill it after it was outside of her, she felt, would be akin to murder.

As Mary wrestled with all these thoughts, she had to talk. Her throat was dry, but she began to make conversation with the others in the room. Soon, among themselves—with a couple veterans of abortion taking the lead—they calmed each other's fears, and reassured themselves that they were doing the only right thing. There was no option. Besides, why feel guilty about something that society, even the law, sanctioned?

Everyone was getting an abortion nowadays. Children were unnecessary nuisances where an individual's career or economics was concerned.

Early the next morning, Mary was given the saline injection. A few hours later, she began labor and was taken to a delivery room, where, only moments before, a mother had joyfully given birth to a baby boy.

The pains were sharp, and Mary was given a local anesthetic. She was still surprised by the intensity of the pain—and the specific nature of it. For more than an hour, the child thrashed about in her womb—nobody had warned her about this—choking and burning in the poison saline solution. But Mary had insisted on not being put under. She felt to do so would be cowardly and frivolous. She wanted to be reasonably scientific and adult about this—to watch the procedure as "it" was removed, discarded from her body.

After the violent kicking had finally ceased, Mary expelled the badly shriveled and crumpled form. A nurse took the fetus and laid it on a towel on another table. Mary could see clearly that the baby was a boy. She could have sworn as the nurse laid him down that he moved his arms and legs. And she was almost certain she heard a soft gurgling sound coming from his throat.

My God! she thought. *He's still alive!*

But before she could say anything, the nurse wrapped the towel firmly around the baby, especially tight around the head.

The doctor began chatting with Mary, telling her how well the procedure had gone and asking how she felt. He explained that they would watch for any unusual bleeding and so on. As Mary listened, her eyes were frozen on the small bundle on the table. She wasn't sure, but she thought there were two or three quick jerks, and then nothing. If the "product" had been alive when it was expelled, by the time the nurses got back to it, it would certainly be dead.

As the nurses took her back to her room, Mary turned her mind off, forcing herself to be rational again.

That night, she fell asleep and began dreaming. In her dream, an innocent infant screamed in agony as its body burned.

Mary awoke, covered in a cold sweat. She got out of bed, walked down the hallway to the pay phone, and called Allen. Soon she had put the dream out of her mind, and she and Allen talked.

The abortion was over, and it was time for her to get on with her life.

After all, she had a career—and an affair—to attend to.

Mary's child was hardly different from Tilka's. Both were offered up as sacrifices to contemporary idols. Tilka's idol was Molech, a product of her society's depraved imagination. Mary's idol was convenience, a product of her society's twisted view of human life.

Both of the sacrificed lives were innocent.

Both societies had decayed to a place where sexual immorality had become the norm.

In both worlds, murder had become commonplace, murder of innocents had become typical, and officially sanctioned murder of innocents had become law.

Both societies were on a crash course with chaos.

GOD'S DREAM

And there these twain upon the skirts of time
Sat side by side, full summ'd in all their powers,
Dispensing harvest, sowing the to-be.
Self-reverent each, and reverencing each;
Distinct in individualities,
But like each other, ev'n as those who love.
>   —Tennyson's "Princess," VII

Human life started with a dream: God's dream.
Its majestic story is found in the simple words of Scripture:

> Then God said, "Let us make man in our image, in our likeness, and let them rule over the fish of the sea and the birds of the air, over the livestock, over all the earth . . . So God created man in His own image, in the image of God he created him; male and female he created them.
>   —Genesis 1:26, 27 NIV

Man's creation was a creation of ultimate excellence, as God took His own image and reproduced it in a very special creature that would be like himself.

In the hand of God the very dust of the earth was transformed into a Man, as God "breathed into his nostrils the breath of life, and man became a living being" (Gen. 2:7 NIV).

The God-implanted character would include a moral, intellectual, and spiritual likeness. Morally, man would have the power of choice, a free will. Intellectually, man would be able to learn, to grow mentally, to discover, to explore, to invent. Spiritually, man would have a capacity to know God, to fellowship with Him, and to live forever.

It would be a relationship of love. Indelibly marked throughout the Scriptures are "For God so loved the world" and "God is love." The corresponding supreme command to man is "Love the Lord your God with all your heart and with all your soul and with all your strength" (Deut. 6:5 NIV).

Man was very special, unique—the only creature with an ultimate destiny. He was made to rule, to have dominion, to be fruitful, to be blessed by God:

> God blessed them and said to them, "Be fruitful and increase in number; fill the earth and subdue it. Rule over the fish of the sea and the birds of the air and over every living creature that moves on the ground. . . . I give you every seed-bearing plant on the face of the whole earth and every tree that has fruit with seed in it. They will be yours for food." And it was so.
>
> —Genesis 1:28-30 NIV

The mark of excellence upon man was affirmed by God after He had completed the entire creation, and just after He had made man: "God saw all that he had made, and it was very good" (Gen. 1:31 NIV).

But in His creation of man, God had a very special gift, an extremely extraordinary gift, to bestow. The heavens He created would not possess it, the plant life would not, the insect life would not, the fish life would not, the animals of the land would not.

Only man!

This gift would so uniquely express God's essential character of life that man would be the only creature who could receive it. For man alone possessed God's moral, intellectual, and spiritual imprint.

The gift would be a love gift because only man had the capacity to love. The gift would be a dream gift because only man had the ability to dream. The gift would be a choice gift because only man had the power to choose. The gift would be a personal gift because only man had the potential for intimacy.

What was this special gift?

It was *the ability to procreate life by an act of will!*

Man was to have implanted in him by the Creator the ability to reproduce life, life that also would have the very image of God.

But it would be life conceived *by choice,* by an exercise of will, by an expression of volition, *by wanting to.*

Animals reproduce, yes; but they do so only by instinct. Their internal programing, put there by God, dictates when they mate, conceive and bear young.

But not man. His gift is unique: he chooses when to bring forth new life. God gave man the unique capacity to create life by an act of will. God created the first life; He formed the gene pool; He then gave man the ability to reproduce life in cooperation with Him—to procreate.

It is wondrous, all a part of the dream!

To say that the significance of this is great is an immeasurable understatement. The implications are awesome—in the unfolding of history, man has populated the entire earth. On this planet, literally billions of persons have been brought to life. This multitude is not a collective, impersonal "mass of humanity," but a collection of unique individuals, each one so absolutely original that no two are the same: each is a rarity of one, each one a masterpiece.

Each is an unrepeatable miracle!

And not only is each person exclusively unique, but each one is especially valuable. This worth is expressed through such care by the heavenly Father that even minute details are recorded—the very hairs on the head of each person are counted, and the record kept up to date (Matt. 10:30). A sparrow cannot die, Jesus pointed out, without the Father noting it. "So don't be afraid," He said, because "you are worth more than many sparrows!" (Matt. 10:31 NIV).

Indeed, Jesus would put each person's eternal worth and uniqueness in perspective when He said, "What good will it be for a man if he gains the whole world, yet forfeits his soul? Or what can a man give in exchange for his soul?" (Matt. 16:26 NIV).

The profoundness of each person's specialness is brought powerfully home when we grasp that every single human being, one by one, has been *given life by the choice* of two other individual human beings, who in turn were given the same life by the choice of two other individual human beings, and on and on and on, all in cooperation with God!

It's the marvel of life, God's gift to His special creation: mankind. You and I!

But when God gave this beautiful gift, He arranged to present it in an unparalleled plan. God would take all the essentials of man's nature He had implanted in man—the moral, the intellectual, the social, the spiritual—and combine these with the sexual genders He had formed: male and female.

The result: Adam, and then Eve, the first two of the race.

It was a joyous time when God fashioned Adam and placed him in Eden, the garden planted by God. Adam was given the oversight of the garden "to work it and take care of it" (Gen. 2:15 NIV).

As Adam went about the work that God had given him, God, according to the story we know so well, saw a need in Adam. God said, "It is not good for the man to be alone. I will make a helper suitable for him" (Gen. 2:18 NIV). Adam was to receive a specially created gift—from God.

Combine all the excitement and happy emotions of every Christmas gift given; join it with the joyous feelings of every beautiful birthday gift ever bestowed; add the bright anticipation of every anniversary, graduation, every occasion whenever a loving gift has been given—and all this does not approach the divine emotion when God made the woman:

> So the Lord God caused the man to fall into a deep sleep; and while he was sleeping, he took one of the man's ribs, and closed up the place with flesh. Then the Lord God made a woman from the rib . . . and he brought her to the man.
>
> —Gen. 2:21, 22 NIV

Adam responded, "This is now bone of my bones and flesh of my flesh; she shall be called 'woman,' for she was taken out of man."

Of the creation of woman, the poet John Milton beautifully wrote in *Paradise Lost*:

Under His forming hands a creature grew,
Man like, but different sex; so lovely fair,
That what seemed fair in all the world, seemed now
Mean, or in her summed up, in her contained,
And in her looks,
Grace was in all her steps, heaven in her eye,
In every gesture dignity and love.

Then, there in the Garden, in the setting of beautiful Eden, God performed the first marriage ever. Before Him stood the man He had given the first life that had His own image, and the woman He had made in love to be the completer of the man. Together they would enter a sacred and joyous union that was so fully intimate they became one flesh and it would be said, "The man and his wife were both naked, and they felt no shame" (Gen. 2:25 NIV.).

Into that special union God placed His gift, the creation of life by an act of will.

The beautiful act to beget new life would be wrapped in the bounds of sacred matrimony. Into this relationship would come two separate wills, a male will and a female will. In their commitment to each other in marriage they would join wills, and have one will. That joint decision would be the coming together to conceive new life in the intimacy of sexual union.

And so man and woman possessed the power to reproduce life—to procreate—by choice, a gift bestowed by God.

The plan of marriage was simply given: "For this reason a man will leave his father and mother and be united to his wife, and they will become one flesh" (Gen. 2:24 NIV).

This Scripture explains that every marriage has two essential parts. One is a public commitment, the other a private consummation. The public commitment is expressed by the scriptural statement, "A man will leave his father and mother and be united to his wife." Every time a man and a woman are to be marrried, they are to declare openly, before the community, their vows. The Christian wedding ceremony is a formalization of this principle.

The requirement for such a public commitment means there is no such thing as a secret marriage; such is a contradiction.

The public commitment itself has two aspects: a leaving and, by contrast, a cleaving. First, there is a leaving of father and mother. The closest relationship apart from marriage is parent and child. But at marriage there is a commitment to an even closer relationship. So the public commitment says that the man and the woman hereby leave the priority of the relationship with parents to form a new primary relationship together. Of course, the leaving of mother and father does not mean a leaving in the sense of honor, but a leaving in the sense of priority. Children, the Scriptures affirm, are always to honor mother and father.

The second aspect of the public commitment is the "vow" aspect—the "cleaving," as the King James Version of the Bible so aptly expresses it. The cleaving is to each other. This is the public declaration of the vows.

The wedding ceremony reflects this: ". . . to have and to hold from this day forward; for better, for worse; for richer, for poorer; in sickness and in health; to love and to cherish; till death do us part, according to God's Holy ordinance; and thereto I plight thee my troth."

Then, besides the public commitment, there is a *private consummation:* ". . . and they will become one flesh."

Following the recital of vows before the community, the

man and the woman alone complete the marriage with sexual union. After the open affirmation of their commitment to each other, the couple privately seal their wedlock in physical oneness.

This oneness is a relationship that is their own creation: the man's maleness, with his entire personality, emotionally, spiritually, socially, and the woman's femaleness, with her complete personality likewise, joined in an act of married love.

And so a man and a woman are married. It was so with Adam and Eve. And into this divinely conceived plan of marriage, complete with all the public and private commitments, shared by the two wills, and complemented by a male and a female—into this, God's unique gift was placed: *the reproduction of life by the exercise of will.* We can join with our Lord when He "saw all that He made, *and it was very good.*"

Some ask, "When does human life begin?"

Does it start at birth? Does it start at mid-gestation when the mother feels the first movements of the baby? Does it start at conception?

Of course we understand what is meant when this question is asked, and how it is to be answered. But, in a majestic sense, God's answer is "No!"

For life had only one beginning, and that was, as we have seen, when God created the first human life, in His image. Into that initial gene pool He placed all the potential for all human life that was to follow.

He gave the procreative right—the right to continue to reproduce that life in cooperation with Him—to Man and Woman, committed for life to each other. Their beautiful, joyous, and loving union by choice would bring forth children, "a heritage from the Lord"! (Ps. 127:3).

Life is sacred! It is to be celebrated!

Such a celebration could be included in the meaning of Jesus when He spoke of the reason for His coming to be our Savior: "I am come that they may have life, and have it more abundantly" (John 10:10 RSV).

We have been given a tremendous gift.

It is part of God's dream. That's where human life started!

But one of the great questions of every civilization has been: What will we do with this gift?

And in the collapse of each society, one can always look back and ask, "What did they do with the Gift?"

THE TWIN SINS

I closed my hands upon a moth,
And when I drew my palms apart,
Instead of dusty, broken wings,
I found a bleeding human heart.

I crushed my foot upon a worm
That had my garden for its goal,
But when I drew my foot aside,
I found a dying human soul.
                    —Dora Sigerson Shorter

We have been given a tremendous gift by God: the capacity to create life by choice. It's all in the majestic area of marriage—and love.

You and I, made in the special image of God, were made to love; to give it, to receive it, to exult in it. Deprived of true love, we perish.

Imagine the most beautiful harbor in the world; perhaps a harbor nestled in a South Pacific island. The verdant mountains slope into the turquoise water. The beach shines with the whitest sand. The water is slippery smooth, broken only by the occasional fish touching the surface for food. It's restful, serene, refreshing to the spirit. Imagine that harbor as your *harbor of love*.

There are special ships that come into that harbor: unique *ships of love*. And there are three of these ships that come into your harbor at various stages of your life.

The first ship is "fellowship." That ship of love arrives at birth and stays throughout life; but it is especially significant in childhood. The fellowship stage of life is when you learn to love everyone; everyone, without regard to status, race, or class.

This is the love of childhood. It is a basic love, the foundation of the others to follow. Those who fail to learn it find the others hard to receive.

Fellowship love is innocent love, without design or selfish intent. It is as a child looking at everyone as made in God's image. The ship is large; it holds everybody.

The second ship is "friendship." This ship of love arrives about adolescence, when a child begins to change, physically and emotionally, into an adult.

The friendship stage of life is when you are attracted to the opposite sex, and you begin to pick out from among them special friends. Dating begins. Love moves toward increased association with particular ones.

This ship is smaller than fellowship, reflecting a growing selectivity. This love is a happy experience, although the time may have trauma.

The third ship is "courtship," and this means a lifelong courtship. This ship arrives at the close of the friendship era, when there is a very special person that has come into your harbor, a person to whom you commit yourself for life in marriage.

This ship is only big enough for two; but it is the most rugged of the three. It is made to sail through anything, face any storm, strike any reef, and never sink.

All this sounds idyllic, but it only emphasizes that life, God-given life, was made to exist in love at all times. We who possess the gift of God's procreative power are to thrive in that life, in love. All three ships were to set sail in innocent love; love that centered on God, knew Him, fellowshiped with Him; love that was untainted by selfishness, by pride, by evil—by sin!

Such an ideal was not to be, as man rebelled against the love of God. Rebellion and love are illustrated by Hosea and his prostituting wife, Gomer. This graphic story shows Israel's rebellion against God's love, and the rebellion of each of us.

Man rebelled, and fell. And in his damning fall, man dragged down every gift God had given him. Man ruined his innocent purity, his moral capacity, his intellect, his spiritual nature—and his procreative gift.

That majestic gift came crashing down, and was trampled underfoot.

In the aftermath of man's rebellion, two insidious sins, fashioned especially by the enemy of man, Satan, vomited themselves out into the lifestyles of man and woman. These two evils had their dark eyes on the special creative gift. Together they would form a deadly duet that would sully, blacken, disfigure and ultimately destroy the beautiful gift. In the process, they would smash the dreams in man and mock God. These two sins would stop at no treachery to accomplish their purpose.

The two evils were immorality and murder. Both would strike at man's beautiful, God-bestowed capacity to create life—and they would strike again and again and again.

Immorality would strike at the creation of life *at* conception. Murder would strike at the creation of life *after* conception.

In this way they would be uniquely related, and so have they ever been. Again and again, the twin sins have attacked the creation of life. They do so today!

Immorality has reared its filthy form under multiple names: fornication, adultery, homosexuality, incest, sodomy, rape, bestiality, pornography, prostitution. But no matter the particular form of this multi-headed sin, it all comes down to one evil, Immorality, whose grand design is to demean God's creative gift.

Immorality blasphemes marriage, into which this gift was placed. It smears the most intimate of human relationships, sexual intercourse, in which this gift functions.

Through child molestation, child pornography, and exposure to adult sins, immorality's selfish passion erases the holy innocence of childhood's fellowship love.

Immorality rips away from developing adolescents the wonder of life and friendship and replaces it with a cynicism borne of involvement in sexual experimentation.

Immorality's insatiable appetite denies adults the deep satisfactions God intended in committed sexual intimacy—that lifelong "courtship" God intended—and keeps them on a treadmill seeking false sensual pleasures.

Our media is filled with immorality; so are our music, our movies, our humor, our values, and on and on.

Immorality's overarching purpose is to strike at the ennobling creation of life in man. And, in so doing, it cheapens life and cheapens man and woman, who are made in God's image.

But then there is the other twin sin which has raised its head: murder. Like immorality, murder is wrapped in selfishness and pride.

And *insensitivity*.

The road to murder is one of insensitivity to the needs of others. Insensitivity has many names: hate, spite, division, violence, cliques, oppression, injustice—even gossip, slander, and backbiting.

Whatever the name, the road of insensitivity leads only to *one culminating point, murder,* whose ultimate purpose—like its twin—is to destroy God's creative gift, and damn mankind!

Murder attacks the helpless, the defenseless, and the innocent. And societies and cultures and nations, from Cain to the present, when they have drifted from God into idolatry—in whatever form—have had a thousand ways of rationalizing their sanction of murder.

The Canaanites, for example, in the name of Molech or Baal, offered their children as sacrifices. Israel and Judah did the same. The ancient city-state of Carthage killed their children by fire. The New Testament Saul, before he was converted and became the apostle Paul, killed Christians in the name of God. Organized religion ravaged believers during the Inquisition. Communism commits genocide in Russia and China in accord with Marxist philosophy. Hitler instituted the Holocaust and the slaughter of six million Jews.

America, and the world, provide abortion on demand.

As a form of murder, abortion is unique in that it is the one form that strikes the creation of life the earliest after conception. It is also the one form that attacks the most helpless of the helpless and the most innocent of the innocent, the unborn children.

Both immorality and murder very often function independently of one another. But whether working at the same time or not, they both demonically attack the creation of life, one at conception, the other after conception.

The Old Testament prophets watched as a nation wandered down the tragic path toward these twin sins. Inspired by God, the prophets saw their beloved Israel and Judah turn aside from their unique covenant relationship with Jehovah and embrace the paganism of the idolatrous cultures around them. They saw Israel and Judah mix the worship of God and Baal. Herbert Schlossberg in *Idols for Destruction* observes this:

> When Israel fell into idolatry, it did not openly renounce the worship of the God of Abraham, Isaac, and Jacob in order to bow before the pagan shrines. Rather, the nation combined the old rituals with what it knew of Canaanite religion. . . . In turning away from God, the nation had not fallen into irreligion, but had combined the temple religion with the pagan beliefs and practices of the surrounding peoples. The worship of the God of the Exodus had been defiled by merging it with the worship of idols.

Then Schlossberg points to the tragic result:

> When judgment finally came to the nation, it fell on this syncretistic perversion.[1]

To this the prophet spoke. As they watched their society leave God and mix paganism with worship of Jehovah, they observed the direction in which idolatry always carries a culture, into a demeaning and destroying of human life: immorality and murder.

The false promise of idolatry is always to elevate man, to allow man to reach his potential, to enjoy pleasure, to forego inconvenience, to liberate.

But it is a lie—a grievous, damning lie. Idolatry *ultimately* enslaves, cheapens, perverts. Its promise of love becomes lust. Its promise of pleasure becomes sexual license. Its promise of understanding becomes insensitivity. Its promise of liberation becomes bondage to self.

Idolatry, whether it be Baalism or secular humanism, is founded upon a rejection of God and the establishing of man as god. It is rooted in human pride, the same attitude of Satan who boasted before he was driven out of the presence of God:

> I will ascend to heaven; I will raise my throne above the stars of God; I will sit enthroned on the mount of the assembly, on the utmost heights of the sacred mountain. I will ascend above the tops of the clouds; I will make myself like the Most High.
>
> —Isa. 14:13-14 NIV

With Satan, idolatry is a rejection of authority, God's holy and loving authority. Every age, every culture, every society, every nation, including ours, has had a crisis of authority: Who will rule? God or idols?

Elijah, the great prophet to Israel during the reign of Ahab and Jezebel, pinpointed this clearly in his famous confrontation with the prophets of Baal and the people—and the whole issue of idolatry—on the hill of Carmel.

"How long will you waver between two opinions?" Elijah thundered. "If the Lord is God, follow him; but if Baal is God, follow him" (1 Kings 18:21 NIV).

On the basis of this challenge by Elijah, Peter Marshall, the former chaplain of the United States Senate and Washington, D.C. pastor, aptly observed that all decisions have a way of coming down to a choice between Baal or

God. That choice between Baal and God, he observed years ago, is America's—and, we might add, Canada's, and Europe's, and humanity's.

Schlossberg writes in *Idols for Destruction:*

> The biblical explanation of the end of societies uses the concept of *judgment.* It depicts them as either having submitted to God or else having rebelled against him. Far from being a typical nationalistic exaltation of a "chosen people," the Old Testament portrays Israel as having become an evil nation, fully deserving the judgment that God meted to it. Its rebellion against God was accompanied by a turning to idols, and this idolatry brought the nation to its end. "With their silver and gold," said the prophet Hosea, "they made idols for their own destruction" (Hosea 8:4 RSV).
>
> Idolatry in its larger meaning is properly understood as any substitution of the created for the creator. People may worship nature, money, mankind, power, history, or social and political systems instead of the God who created them all.[2]

The prevailing idolatry of our age is secular humanism, and it contains all the elements of idolatry.

The truth of this statement is borne out by the living evidence before us that it is producing the same kind of culminating sins that other idolatries have produced: gross immorality and legally sanctioned murder. These twin sins attack viciously God's great gift, the creation of life.

One question before us is: Where will our idolatry take us? The idolatries of past ages, if not repented of, led to judgment—as we shall examine in more detail.

What about us?

There are many shortages today, of energy, natural resources, clear air and water. But could the greatest shortage be the shortage of time? Time to repent and once again honor God as our Lord? Time to affirm, once again, as a nation, "In God We Trust"?

Notes for Chapter Four

1 Herbert Schlossberg, *Idols for Destruction*, Thomas Nelson, 1983, pp. 233-34.
2 Ibid., p. 6.

THE CULTURE OF MURDER

> See how the faithful city has become a harlot!
> She once was full of justice; righteousness used
> to dwell in her—but now murderers!
> —Isaiah 1:21 NIV

To help answer the question "Where will our idolatry take us?" we can ask another question: "Where have idolatries taken cultures in the past?"

Over and over again in the past, in culture after culture, the twin sins of murder and immorality, which attack God's creative gift, have arisen; they are the product of forgetting God and replacing worship of Him with idolatry.

Among the many places in the Scriptures we could go to find an answer, one especially helpful and graphic place is the story of Hosea.

Hosea lived in an idolatrous, immoral and murderous generation. He was led by God to marry Gomer, who became a very promiscuous woman, and this marriage became a dramatic and gripping "visual aid" for his prophecies.

Gomer's unfaithfulness was a vivid picture used by God

39

to illustrate Israel's spiritual unfaithfulness, how she had forgotten God and embraced idolatry—and idolatry's sins.

Israel's judgment was portrayed by Gomer's decline into prostitution, and Gomer's rescue by Hosea reflected God's ultimately forgiving attitude toward Israel. As a result of his personal anguish, Hosea's message to Israel was dynamic and to the point.

In fact, everything in Hosea's personal life is a symbol of God's message to Israel. Even Hosea's children and their names are part of the message. He named their first child Jezreel, as a sign of judgment over the valley of Jezreel, the dwelling place of the Israelites. The second child was named Lo-Ruhamah, meaning No Mercy. And the final child was named Lo-Ammi, meaning Not My People.

Chapters one through three of Hosea are a capsule version of the cycle of God's judgment and forgiveness for Israel, set against the relationship of Hosea and Gomer. Then, in chapter four, having lived this vivid "visual aid," Hosea begins his strong indictment of Israel in earnest. He takes on the role of the forceful prosecuting attorney, and in the language of the courtroom graphically speaks the Word of God, pointing out the crimes of Israel.

> Hear the word of the Lord,
> You children of Israel,
> For the Lord brings a charge
>   against the inhabitants of the land:
>
> There is no truth or mercy
> Or knowledge of God in the land.
> By swearing and lying,
> Killing and stealing and committing adultery,
> They break all restraint,
> *With bloodshed after bloodshed.* [italics added]

Verse 2 is the crucial portion of the passage:

> Therefore the land will mourn;
> And everyone who dwells there will waste away
> With the beasts of the field
> And the birds of the air;
> Even the fish of the sea will be taken away. . . .
>
> Harlotry, wine, and new wine enslave the heart.
> My people ask counsel from their wooden idols,
> And their staff informs them.
> For the spirit of harlotry has caused them to stray,
> And they have played the harlot against their God.
> They offer sacrifices on the mountaintops,
> And burn incense on the hills,
> Under oaks, poplars, and terebinths,
> Because their shade is good.
> Therefore your daughters commit harlotry,
> And your brides commit adultery.
> —Hosea 4:1-3, 11-13 NKJV

What happened to the Israelites to bring them so far from their covenant relationship with God? They became victims of the culture around them, gradually seduced by pagan worship. This was due in large part to the fact that there were distinct similarities between the pagan rites and Israel's worship. As David Payne writes in *Kingdoms of the Lord,* "One can appreciate . . . that many an ordinary Israelite could see little harm in Canaanite religious practices, and perhaps little essential difference in them. When he did observe distinctions, moreover, he may have been tempted to think that the Canaanites had the better of it, since they were such gifted and civilized people. Was Yahweh perhaps the god of the deserts outside Palestine, with little power or influence in Canaan?[1]

Yet, despite similarities in worship, there were glaring contrasts between the theologies of Israel and Canaan. Foremost was Israel's strict monotheism as opposed to Canaan's polytheism. While the Israelites revered Yahweh, the pagan worship embraced a myriad of gods and goddesses.

For example, while Baal was prominent in the pagan rites (he was the god of thunder and rain, rain being a crucial element in their agricultural economy), El was the senior deity. The Canaanites considered him their creator god. And Baal's father was Dagon, the god of vegetation and corn.

Goddesses included Ashtoreth, consort to El; Asherah; and Anat, Baal's companion. All are mentioned in the Old Testament and were goddesses of fertility.

What was happening to Israel as they became more deeply involved in pagan practices?

They were losing, as Payne puts it, "the sense of God's unique majesty and of his systematic, orderly, purposeful intentions for his people." The Canaanites were most concerned about abundant harvests—in much the same way that we modern Americans are concerned about our individual affluence and, on a larger scale, the general economy.

"The plight of peasant-farmers when Palestine was afflicted by drought and disease of crops was indeed desperate," Payne points out. "Small wonder, then, that they isolated 'corn' as one deity, and 'fertility' as another. In seeking to worship Dagon and the fertility goddesses, they were in effect trying to understand the forces of nature, and secondly trying to control these forces. To harness them, they felt, one must first of all be on good terms with the appropriate deities, by sacrifices, offerings and rituals, and then proceed to co-operate with those deities. The latter purpose could be achieved—as they thought—by the practice of what we now call 'sympathetic' or 'imitative' magic. Knowing nothing scientific about the reproduction and growth of plants, they envisaged these processes in terms of human sexual relations (as did many ancient peoples). To secure the fertility of the ground, therefore, Baal and his consort Anat were depicted as having sexual intercourse; and it is certain that in Canaanite rites the worshippers emulated the gods, believing that such conduct would promote the good harvests they so much desired. Accordingly, each Canaanite shrine had its cult-prostitutes, both male and female.

"The Canaanite faith, then, can be characterized as a fertility religion. . . . For the Israelites to turn to the fertility cult, therefore, was not merely to renounce morality and ethics, but to reject the covenant and all that it implied."[2]

The immoral fertility cult devalued and debased human beings, and its pervasive influence throughout Palestine was of special concern to the Old Testament prophets. When they accused fellow Israelites of "playing the harlot" with foreign deities, the metaphor was extremely well chosen—more literal than metaphorical, in fact.

But sexual promiscuity wasn't the most frightening aspect of pagan worship. It was only one of two "twin sins" that destroyed Israel. The other one undermined the value and dignity of human life even more: human sacrifice. The prophets were horrified by this practice, which was carried out in honor of the pagan god Molech, "the King" (also translated Milcom or Melek, or otherwise known as Chemosh, Athtar, or Shalem).[3]

The commentary on Hosea by Anderson and Freedman describes the situation thus:

Idolatrous and apostate worship has two outstanding features, on both of which the prophet pours out his vehemence. Sexual promiscuity in the fertility cult undermines the moral structure of the covenant, and is a gross violation of the basic requirements of community life under God. Furthermore it leads in some circuitous way to *the culminating sin against God and people, that is the shedding of innocent blood*. This is not ordinary murder, itself an ultimate crime, *but officially sanctioned human sacrifice.*[4]

As if the shedding of blood were not horrible enough, the Canaanites—and eventually the Israelites—shed *innocent* blood, and did it by *official sanction,* as a habit of their society.

The Israelites still knew *that* God was, but they had forgotten *who* God was. They lost an intimate knowledge of God's unique, true character and love. The Israelites fell into a combined error of falsely worshiping the true God and truly worshiping false gods—they were guilty of both apostasy and idolatry. This double error in their religious worship led them to the twin sins of sexual immorality and murder.

As we study the time of Hosea, we can note the similarities between the pagan culture surrounding Israel—and Judah later as well—and the culture of secular humanism surrounding us today, a culture that has rejected the knowledge of God.

Others have noticed it too. A *Christianity Today* editorial observes, "Actually, the real question is not simply whether a man believes in God (this is a sound beginning, according to Hebrews 11:6) but whether he knows him. . . . There is no doubt that many men today have lost the sense of God's presence and the certainty of knowledge about him. . . . But the reason is not so much a change in man's environment and outlook as it is a deliberate rejection of the ground on which God may be found."[5]

Our society has shifted, slowly but surely, from a God-centered viewpoint to a self-centered base: God-denying humanism.

No longer does man look outside himself for answers and meaning, but he looks even deeper within. As a result, his awareness of God fades, and he is left with nothing inside himself to discover except emptiness and despair.

This then leads him to the conclusion that man is the result of nothing-plus-nothing, as Francis Schaeffer states it, merely a stopping point on the line of chance and evolution that began with an amoeba and will end who knows where.

This self-centeredness has its roots in the beginnings of humanity, as Craig Ellison states in "The Roots of Loneliness," which appeared in *Christianity Today:*

> When sin entered into human experience, the basic bond between man and God was broken. From the point Adam and Eve chose to violate their relationship with God they became self-centered and narcissistic. Human experience became forever marked by a divisive self-centeredness. . . .
>
> The removal of God as the center of human relationship was the precursor of today's secularization. In order to cope with sin without repenting, modern man has attempted to get rid of God by pronouncing him dead.

But this attempt plunges man deeper into the depths of loneliness and despair without remedy. . . . The secular person casts about for substitutes that will allow him to retain his narcissism but overcome his loneliness and alienation. Drugs, alcohol, sex, and marathon encounter experiences become part of the search, as do T.M. and countless other semi-religious, semi-psychological trips.[6]

This is the same situation in which the Israelites found themselves. Having lost their vision of the true God, they sought meaning in the rites of pagan worship, which became nothing more than state-sanctioned immorality and murder. Their experimentation with paganism was the same thing as today's society searching for meaning in God-ignoring secularism.

Yet this godless narcissism has an unexpected twist, which is simply the logical extension of the evolution/mechanistic mindset produced by a humanistic world view. Carl F.H. Henry, noted theologian, cited this dilemma in *Christianity Today:*

What now dominates the intellectual arena is a naturalistic evolutionary philosophy or a radically secular view of reality and life.

This antisupernaturalistic, anti-God development ought to chill our souls. Neither a utopian evolutionary philosophy nor a radically secular alternative can persuasively maintain the case for human rights. A merely evolutionary view of human origins and development cannot vindicate either the permanent or the universal dignity of mankind. Bertrand Russell reminded us many decades ago that if we take evolution seriously, no reason remains for attaching finality to man. Strict regard for evolution implies the future emergence of a still higher form from which standpoint man as he currently exists will be as insignificant as is the primal protozoa as viewed by man, which is declared to have risen from it. In short, philosophical evolution cannot guarantee the permanent dignity of the human species. . . .

The radically secular notion that ethical imperatives are nothing but self-serving postulates that promote individual fulfillment clouds the meaning of truth and of human rights and duties. An evolutionary or relativistic philosophy can preserve no unrevisable agenda of human rights, if indeed it has any rule whatever for "rights" in distinction from self-interest. The loss of God as the source, sanction, and stipulation of human rights befogs the precise identification of human rights.[7]

This shift in viewpoint to regarding man as a "cosmic accident" is espoused by secularists on every side. In science, one of humanism's foremost spokesmen is Carl Sagan, and he preaches his doctrine of Godless creation and life through the powerful voice of the media. His Public Broadcasting System (PBS) series *Cosmos* has become highly popular. Many other PBS series also espouse a particularly secular point of view, and even go so far as to flatly deny the legitimacy of any other but a secular worldview.

This basic philosophical and theological shift has

affected more than just television. It has affected the very fabric of society. People, bombarded by the secular message in movies, books, music and television, behave less like people and more like cosmic accidents, without regard for other humans. Even violence in our society has changed.

Robert Vernon, assistant chief of police in Los Angeles, California, noted this change in an article in *Christianity Today:*

> Historically, there has been a relationship between the murderer and his victim—a jealous husband, a disgruntled employee, an angry business partner. Now, however, we are witnessing more murders that occur for the sheer thrill of the kill itself, or as a flippant means to settle an argument. A wanton disregard for the value of life would appear to be on the increase. In more homicide cases today the victim and perpetrator are strangers, completely unrelated to one another. In many of these cases, there appears to be little the victim could have done to prevent the crime.[8]

In other words, if there is no meaning to life (no God, only a mechanistic, impersonal universe to contend with), then life has no value except to oneself. The social ethic has degenerated to where "I am valuable to me, but you are not, except as I can use you to achieve my goals."

This is the same type of situation that Israel faced as she fell deeper into pagan worship, the equivalent to secular humanism in the eighth century B.C. Sexual immorality was rampant, condoned by the "church" and state. Murder and insensitivity were common. Look again at that concise indictment in Hosea 4:

> There is no truth or mercy
> Or knowledge of God in the land.
> By swearing and lying,
> Killing and stealing and committing adultery,
> They break all restraint,
> With bloodshed after bloodshed.
> —Hosea 4:1, 2 NKJV

The parallels betwen our society today and Israel's in the eighth century B.C. are shocking. This passage of Scripture could easily describe our modern culture.

Society has rejected a true knowledge of God. Even our national leaders have been caught, involved in scandals of all sorts. Every day the news brings stories of heinous crimes of murder, torture and abuse. Sexual immorality is widespread, even accepted and encouraged, through our magazines, movies, and television programs.

But, as horrible as all this was in Israel's time (and is now), it wasn't the single cause of their downfall. There was more, and it was in this final, horrifying element that I discovered the most shocking parallel between our two cultures—a parallel that sobers, and should move us to take action.

The shocking parallel involved Israel's *other* sin—the sin of murder.

Let's look at murder. We can show that this terrible sin involves three levels in any culture. This is really not hard to understand, as our courts have always made a vital distinction between, say, manslaughter (also distinguished as voluntary or involuntary) and first- and second-degree murder. The Old Testament law made similar distinctions.

Essentially what our system of law does is say that the degree of murder is determined by the amount of premeditation that goes into the criminal act. We say that a person who kills another accidentally has a different degree of guilt than a person who commits open, calculated, planned murder. The latter is guilty of homicide in the first degree and is deserving of the ultimate penalty, which can include execution.

When we come to murder as it is accepted and practiced by a culture or nation, we can discern three levels. Note the distinctions.

The first level is common murder, people killing people, the kind we see reported in the news every day.

The second level, though just as deadly, has an added element. It involves the murder of the helpless or innocents. In one sense, of course, all murder victims are helpless and innocent, but for our purposes here the helpless and innocent include the poor, the aged, the infirm, children, widows, babies—those too weak to defend themselves. This is a vicious, damning form of murder.

In the Scriptures, God takes up the case on the side of the helpless and innocent. For instance, Scripture says, "Do not deny justice to your poor people in their lawsuits. Have nothing to do with a false charge and do not put an innocent or honest person to death, for I will not acquit the guilty" (Exod. 23:6-7 NIV).

But then there is the third level, which is an extension of the first and second levels. This level is the most heinous form of murder, the most deserving of judgment.

This third level is murder of innocents by official sanction.

For a society, it is calculated, premeditated, planned murder. It is societal first-degree murder.

The third level of murder represents in God's eyes a culminating step in a culture's descent into spiritual degeneracy. In Israel's and Judah's time, this kind of murder occurred in the form of the sacrifice of innocent infants to the pagan gods. The firstborn child was placed on a fiery altar and cruelly burned to death in the service of the pagan deities.

As we look around us today, we might ask, What parallels to such barbarism might be found in our culture? When have modern men murdered innocent, defenseless victims by official sanction?

Hitler's insidious slaughter of millions of Jews comes easily to mind, of course. Few would argue the immorality and insensitive cruelty exhibited by the Nazis in their death camps.

But what about more recent examples? Are there parallels of such violence occurring in this day? In this year? Is there innocent blood being shed even now, by official sanction?

Is the spirit of Molech with us now?

Could there exist a culture of murder—today?

Notes for Chapter Five

1 David Payne, *Kingdom of the Lord*, Eerdmans, 1981, p. 202.

2 Ibid., pp. 203-204.

3 Ibid., pp. 204-205.

4 Anderson & Freedman, *Hosea*, Doubleday, 1980, p. 49.

5 James Dobson, "Theism and the Modern Mind," *Christianity Today*, January 19, 1968, p. 49.

6 Craig Ellison, "The Roots of Loneliness," *Christianity Today*, March 10, 1978.

7 Carl F.H. Henry, "Human Rights and Wrongs," *Christianty Today*, July 8, 1977.

8 Robert Vernon, "Unearthing the Roots of Violence in America," *Christianity Today*, August 6, 1982.

A WAR OF WORDS

The crowning irony of this thoroughly immoral age is that more than perhaps any other it is incessantly and unapologetically moralistic. There is nothing so brutal that it cannot be defended with the joyous trumpeting of self-righteous satisfaction. An invasion is called an act of love; destroying a village is an act of salvation; reducing a poor man to perpetual dependence or killing an infant an act of compassion. There are few miserable little despots who do not use this language.
—Herbert Schlossberg, *Idols for Destruction*

Under the headline "Abortions Reach Record High in 1980," the *Information Please Almanac 1983* runs this startling paragraph:

About one of every four pregnancies in the United States ended in abortion in 1980 according to a survey conducted by the Alan Guttmacher Institute. Some 1.55 million abortions were performed, more than double the 744,000 legal abortions performed in 1973, the first year of legalized abortions. A shift from the birth control pill and intrauterine devices for health reasons was a significant factor in the increase, according to statisticians at the institute.[1]

Since its legalization in 1973, abortion has become a prime method of birth control. Abortion on demand is simply a matter of convenience. The unborn child is just another discardable, disposable "thing." In fact, according to John Powell, S.J., "In the United States it is statistically confirmed that the most dangerous place for anyone to be, with regard to the preservation of one's life, is in the womb of one's mother."[2] The womb is the free-fire zone!

The real stampede toward abortion began on January 22, 1973, when the Supreme Court of the United States legalized abortion. Here is a summary of that decision as quoted from *Roe v. Wade*, Justice Blackmun delivering the opinion of the Court:

(a) For the stage prior to approximately the end of the first trimester, the abortion decision and its effectuation must be left to the medical judgment of the pregnant woman's attending physician.

(b) For the stage subsequent to approximately the end of the first trimester, the State, in promoting its interest in the health of the mother, may, if it chooses, regulate the abortion procedure in ways that are reasonably related to maternal health.

(c) For the stage subsequent to viability, the State, in promoting its interest in the potentiality of human life, may, if it chooses, regulate, and even proscribe, abortion except where it is necessary, in appropriate medical judgment, for the preservation of the life or health of the mother.

What the Justices of the Supreme Court managed to do in that single decision was to trash centuries of social tradition, decades of scientific evidence, and great expanses of the scriptural foundation for American life. They ignored the ethics of a majority of Americans at the time. They struck down the abortion laws of all fifty states. They made abortion on demand, at virtually every stage of pregnancy, the law of the land. All of which "gave the United States the dubious distinction of having the most permissive abortion laws of any nation in the Western World."[3]

In subsequent rulings, the Court has decided that a wife need not obtain her husband's consent for an abortion, and neither does a minor need her parent's consent for an abortion.

How has this happened? How have so many been seduced by so few into allowing such laws to be enacted, even when these laws do not represent the majority view?

It should be noted here, too, that biblical morality does not need to be accepted by a majority to be right. God's law is God's law, regardless of whether the majority accepts it or not. There are times when even a minority opinion is the right opinion, although this has not necessarily been the case in the development of abortion legislation.

For one thing, we have confused "legal" with "ethical." Abortion, or any sin, is not made ethical or right, even though it is made legal.

But moreover, the problem is rooted in semantics. *America has lost sight of the wrongness of abortion largely because it has become mired in a war of words, lost in a semantic smokescreen that clouds the real issues.*

Early on in the debate over abortion, the issue became the target of subtle semantic swordplay. Words became disproportionately important because abortion was such an emotional issue. As sides began to form, each also began choosing terms very carefully—for the words were bound to be the ammunition for this battle. Both pro-abortionists and anti-abortionists have become caught up in this insidious, subtle battle of words—and both have essentially missed the real issues because of it.

At the beginning of the debate, it was very simple to determine which side was which. Those who favored liberal abortion laws were termed *pro*-abortionists. Those who opposed abortion were termed *anti*-abortionists. The difference was as clear as black and white. The unborn child was called an unborn child, or a fetus. While *fetus* wasn't as emotive as *unborn child,* it was recognizable enough to evoke a clear image of what was being discussed. When the term *fetus* is mentioned, most people picture an unborn infant.

To have an abortion meant simply and clearly to kill an unborn child, or to destroy a fetus. The image was clear and graphic. Even more so since science had, in recent years, allowed us to actually observe life inside the womb. We were entranced by the miracle of life as it was taking place where no one had before been able to look. It was awe-inspiring to see how human the tiny fetus actually looked, even at only a few weeks.

And this was the problem for the pro-abortionists. They realized that, as things stood, they were fighting a losing battle. As long as such images were coming to mind every time abortion was debated, how could anyone agree to kill another human being, regardless of how small it might be?

The abortionists needed new terms, that while still being somewhat emotive, painted their cause in a more semantically positive light.

The anti-abortionists had already taken the semantic offensive by terming their movement the *pro-life* movement. To be anti-abortion meant to be pro-life. And that was a tough argument for the abortionists to disprove—until they created new terms and diversionary issues.

First, they changed the name of their movement, taking their cue from the pro-lifers, and invented the term *pro-choice*. The term is strongly feminist, and emphasizes the rights of the mother over the rights of the unborn infant.

Theologian R.C. Sproul[4] zeroes in on this deceiving choice of words:

> Two vital questions must be faced by those wrestling with *the premier moral issue of our day*. The first question is, "What is the practical difference between pro-abortion and pro-choice?" In terms of legislation, a vote for pro-choice is a vote for pro-abortion, which the pro-abortionists understand clearly.

Then Sproul shows that this has clearly influenced public opinion:

> No one knows the exact figures, but it is obvious from the polls that a large group of voters, if not a plurality of them, favor the middle ground. Certainly it is this middle position that has swung the balance of

legislative power and the weight of public opinion to the side of the pro-abortionist.

We hear it said repeatedly, "I would not choose to have an abortion, but I think every woman has a right to make that choice for herself.

Argument Number One by the pro-abortionists is the so-called pro-choice "rights argument."

Next, to further strengthen their position and the rightness of their emphasis on the mother's rights, they had to create the impression that the unborn infant wasn't deserving of rights. How did they do this? By bringing in the term *viability.*

Argument Number Two by the pro-abortionists is the "viability" argument.

Viability refers to the fetus' ability to live or survive outside the womb. In other words, until the fetus develops to the point that it would be able to live outside the womb if it were born at that moment, it is not "viable"—not a viable human being, in the thinking of the pro-abortionists, and therefore worthy of being aborted.

They have also coined the phrase "product of conception," or the medical industry's abbreviation "POC." This term effectively strips the fetus of any real living status. It dehumanizes the whole abortion process, making the fetus an "it," a "thing," a "collection of cells," a "mass of tissue," "protoplasmic rubbish," and even a "gobbet of meat."

Essentially, then, the pro-abortionists have stated their case so that a woman has the right—since it's her body—to abort whenever a fetus is unviable or unwanted.

Argument Number Three by the pro-abortionists is the "wantedness" issue.

An unwanted child can mean several things. The poor are typically earmarked by pro-abortionists as those who most want and need abortions, because they don't want—and can't afford—babies. But "it is not the poorer people who are the main proponents of abortion," says Kevin Perrotta, managing editor of *Pastoral Renewal*. "Gallup has shown that abortion on demand is much more strongly favored by whites than blacks, by upper-income than lower-income folks, and by business and professional people than manual laborers."[5]

If not poor, a couple could be so self-centered, so caught up in their careers, that they've decided they have no room in their lives for a child, aware that the option of abortion as birth-control is always there.

But another, more tragic case of "unwantedness" stems from science's advances in early pregnancy diagnostic techniques. Today, it is possible to determine at very early stages of pregnancy whether or not the child is "normal." In other words, it can be detected if there is any disease, deformity, or other physical disorder in the unborn child. As a result, when a mother today discovers her unborn child could or will be born "defective," she often chooses to discard that imperfect child through abortion.

So, the pro-abortionists claim (1) that every woman has ultimate *rights* over her own body, (2) the unborn fetus is not human life until it is determined to be *viable*, and (3) that every child must be a wanted child—and every woman can discard an *unwanted* child as if tossing away a paper towel.

The Pro-Choice "Rights" Argument

The pro-choice "rights" issue stems from the original *Roe v. Wade* case. There are two important considerations to keep in mind concerning the landmark case. First, the case did not develop from an individual seeking to have an abortion at the time of the ruling. Jane Roe was the fictitious name given to the plaintiff, Norma McCorvey. McCorvey was approached by two Texas Law School classmates, newly graduated from law school and avidly interested in the challenge of striking down Texas' law that banned most abortions. They actually put out the word among their colleagues that they were looking for a client that would fit their needs!

The lawyers, Linda Coffee and Sarah Weddington, discovered McCorvey and decided she was perfect for their needs. McCorvey at the time was a twenty-five-year-old divorced waitress. She had become pregnant as the result of a gang rape. Too poor to leave Texas for a legal abortion elsewhere, she sued the state. Unable to get the abortion she wanted, she subsequently delivered the baby and gave the infant up for adoption. The child, a girl, was already four years old by the time the Supreme Court handed down the infamous ruling in 1973.

The second consideration is that, in the case of *Roe v. Wade*, a specific situation was used as a general standard, and the resulting judgment is accordingly flawed. Not every abortion is the result of gang rape. Yet the judgment on a case involving a gang rape has now allowed abortion in every instance. A bizarre twist of logic, to say the least.

One pro-abortionist's statement demonstrates how one argument is used to support another—in this case, the viability argument is assumed, and, along with other clever word tricks, is used to support the "rights" argument (italics mine):

> The fetus is alive. It takes little knowledge of
> biology to recognize this fact. However, the

biological fact of life does not necessarily require that the *cells* in question be awarded full rights under the Constitution.

A human embryo is a *collection of human cells* with the *potential* for developing into an independent human being. However, the fact is that a fetus or embryo in the *pre-viable stage* is incapable of survival outside the body of another human being.[6]

The statement also makes the same mistake as the *Roe v. Wade* ruling, using a narrow and unusual situation to pass judgment on the whole abortion issue:

We have a very strong judicial tradition of respect for the *sanctity* of each citizen's body. Surgery and other medical procedures are not performed on patients against their will or that of their guardians. If I were dying of renal failure and you had the only compatible kidneys in the world that might save my life, no American court would force you to donate one to me, even if you were somehow responsible for my kidney ailment.

Yet to require a pregnant woman to share her body unwillingly with a pre-viable embryo is an even more appalling usurpation of her right to security in her own person. Let us not carry our concern for the unborn to the point of unconscionable abandonment of cherished rights of the already-born.[7]

One of the disturbing contradictions in the "rights" argument is that the same people who insist on a mother's right to murder her unborn baby will cry out for the rights of a convicted murderer, insisting that capital punishment is cruel and barbaric. They call for life for the guilty, but call for death for the innocent.

Essentially, then, "pro-choice" really means "pro-convenience." The "rights" argument is a smokescreen. We cherish rights in America, and rightly so—but unbalanced by morality and the knowledge of God, those rights become idols.

And so they have become in America today.

Rights are only one side of our great heritage. The teeter-totter is balanced with "responsibility." Without such a balance, our rights could lead to our last rites.

As is usually the case, society confuses law with morality. Anything legal is assumed to be moral. This type of thinking is reasonable if there is no God, as secular humanists believe. Without God, man is the measure of all things, and man's laws are his only moral determinants. But man is not truly the measure of all things. God is. And God's laws are absolutes which cannot be legislated away.

Sproul writes, "As Christians we recognize, I hope, that there is a profound difference between a moral right and a legal right. Ideally, legal rights reflect moral rights, but such is not always the case."

Then he adds, "How does one establish the moral right to choose abortion? From the law of nature? From the law of God? Hardly. Natural law abhors abortion and divine law implicitly condemns it."[8]

Even though society's lawmakers determine the society's morality, society is often still squeamish about moving away from God's laws—and that uneasy society needs further rationalization to assuage any tell-tale guilt. Such is the case with abortion.

Sproul points to this:

The unspoken assumption of the right-to-choice position is the assumption that I am free to choose whatever I want—an assumption repugnant to both God and nature. I never have the moral right to do evil. I may have the civil and legal right to sin but not the moral right. The only moral rights I have are to righteousness. . . .

If abortion on demand is evil, no one has the moral right to choose it. If it is an offense against life, the government must not permit it. The day is being captured by the moderate middle who have not faced the ethical implications of this position. . . .

And then Sproul cuts to the center of the issue of pro-choice:

This is the moral cop-out of our day—the shame of our churches and her leaders. It is time to get off the fence. Pro-choice is pro-abortion. Be clear about that and abandon the muddled middle.

Sproul of course is right, and may we take a cue from his sharp analysis and realize that the current tragic attempt by pro-abortionists to hide behind the smokscreen of pro-choice is a deadly neutrality. Such fence-sitting consigns to death millions of unborn citizens each year.

The allure that pro-choice has to public and religious leaders is that the position sounds very democratic, very correct for our pluralistic culture. It is the perfect out for a lawmaker, enabling him or her to come down foursquare on both sides of the issue. In legislative debates, it carries the day.

However, such double-mindedness is biblically indefensible. Can we not hear Elijah come thundering into our culture, and, standing before pro-choice politicians and priests, strongly call in those words referred to earlier: "How long halt you between two opinions? If God is God, serve Him; but if Baal is God, serve Him!"

The spirit of Elijah is needed today upon churchman and citizen to call our culture to quit the mixed signal of pro-choice; and to assert that to be such is effectively to be pro-abortion, and no amount of semantic tiptoeing can alter that reality.

It is time to tell our legislators that hiding behind pro-choice is a grievous, tragic decision by them to stand by and allow the sanction of the shedding of innocent blood continue unchallenged.[9]

Although abortion has been legalized, the battle still rages. The pro-abortionists are still having a difficult time erasing that image of a developing human from everyone's minds. We've seen the pictures in the magazines and on television, and we know that a fetus, even only a few weeks old, resembles a miniature human being—he already looks like the person he is! So, the abortionists plunge ahead in the battle over semantics with the idea of viability.

The "Viability" Argument

Terms used in the pro-abortion editorial cited above—"pre-viable embryo" is a classic example—are common now when abortionists are referring to unborn babies. Through semantics, they are attempting to dehumanize the tiny life. Common terms include "embryo," "tissue," "clump of cells," "it," and "product of conception."

The term *fetus* is still used, though only when the description creates a negative impression as associated with other terms.

A tragic kind of question is now being asked: When does a clump of cells actually become an infant, a child—a human being? That is the battle raging right now, one in which the anti-abortionists have unwittingly become caught up.

When does life begin in the womb? Obstetrician Bernard Nathanson once ran a large abortion clinic in New York but has completely changed his views and is now a fervent anti-abortionist. He writes:

> Using new technology, we can see that the fetus behaves like any and all of us. If you make a loud sound, its heart speeds up; if you poke it with a needle, it jumps. It is the accumulation of these human qualities, responses, appearance, and for all we know, psychology, that convince me that this is in fact human life.

Dr. Christopher Tietze, senior consultant for the Population Council of New York, tragically links the value of life to the viability issue. He does concede that "biological life of the individual begins at the union of ovum and sperm," but them lamentably observes:

> . . . At what point does this life deserve the respect and protection that we accord people? Such respect and protection become appropriate when the fetus has attained viability, that is when it has become capable of surviving and eventually maintaining a meaningful, independent life. At present,

viability is assumed by most doctors to be reached at about 24 weeks from the onset of the last menstrual period. However, some genetic defects, such as anencephaly, where a brainless newborn will die within minutes or hours, and Tay-Sachs disease, where a child will die after long suffering at two to five years, may not be discovered until late in pregnancy. Is such a fetus viable; is that meaningful life? I think not.

Others deny the ability of science to answer the question at all. Yale University's Dr. Leon Rosenberg, chairman of the department of human genetics in the School of Medicine, said:

This is such a metaphysical concept. Of course, a new life is generated when the egg is fertilized by the sperm; but the ovum is already a living cell, and so is the sperm. I know of no scientific evidence which bears on the questions of when actual human life exists. Science, per se, doesn't deal with the complex quality called "humanness" any more than it does with such equally complex concepts as love, faith or trust. Without experiments there is no science, no way to prove or disprove any idea. I maintain that concepts such as humanness are beyond the purview of science because no idea about them can be tested experimentally.

Some say, as Dr. Tietze suggests, that a fetus is not viable outside the womb until after twenty-four hours or longer. Such is the muddle in the war of words over "viability," a grievous debate that should never have occurred. That the Christian community has even entered into the debate shows that even the church lacks a knowledge of God's character and of His great, creative gift to man and woman made in His image.

But in addition to spiritual concerns, just from a medical standpoint, viability is being challenged as great strides continue to be made in medicine. Prematurely born infants are being kept alive at earlier and earlier stages of development.

And then another question is coming chillingly to the forefront, an issue that is causing more than one doctor and nurse and potential mother a great amount of personal anguish: What do you do when a fetus, which has been determined to be "unviable," is aborted alive?

What do you do? And live abortions are becoming a greater problem as more of them accidentally occur. Standing there and watching an aborted baby die is a tremendously traumatic experience, to say the least.

What are we doing to ourselves?

In an appendix to his excellent book *A Time for Anger*,[10] Franky Schaeffer includes a striking article by reporters Liz Jeffries and Rick Edmonds entitled "Abortion." The article first appeared in the *Philadelphia Inquirer* on August 2, 1981. It is a lengthy account of the problems of live abortions, and the corresponding problems of doctors who are performing abortions. It is a remarkable piece of journalism in that no side is taken, and the ethical questions concerning abortion are very clearly raised.

The article opens with this account:

> A woman's scream broke the late-night quiet and brought two young obstetrical nurses rushing to

Room 4456 of the University of Nebraska Medical Center. The patient, admitted for an abortion, had been injected 30 hours earlier with a salt solution, which normally kills the fetus and causes the patient to deliver a mass of lifeless tissue, in a process similar to a miscarriage.

This time, though, something had gone wrong. When nurse Marilyn Wilson flicked on the lights and pulled back the covers, she found, instead of the stillborn fetus she'd expected, a live 2½-pound baby boy, crying and moving his arms and legs there on the bed.

Dismayed, the second nurse, Joanie Fuchs, gathered the squirming infant in loose bedcovers, dashed down the corridor and called to the other nurses for help. She did not take the baby to an intensive care nursery, but deposited it instead on the stainless steel drainboard of a sink in the maternity unit's Dirty Utility Room—a large closet where bedpans are emptied and dirty linens stored. Other nurses and a resident doctor gathered and gaped.

Finally, a head nurse telephoned the patient's physician, Dr. C.J. LaBenz, at home, apparently waking him.

"He told me to leave it where it was," the head nurse testified later, "just to watch it for a few minutes, that it would probably die in a few minutes."

This was in Omaha, in September 1979. It was nothing new. Hundreds of times a year in the United States, an aborted fetus emerges from the womb alive and kicking. Some survive. A baby girl in Florida, rescued by nurses who found her lying in a bedpan, is 5 years old now and doing well. The Omaha baby lasted barely 2½ hours after he was put in the closet with the dirty linen.

The article continues, reporting that it is estimated 400 to 500 live abortions occur every year in the U.S., making it a daily occurrence. And for every case that is reported, dozens, even hundreds, probably go unreported. For when such an incident comes to light, someone often attempts to prosecute those involved. But there have yet to be any convictions.

The debate concerning viability, then, degenerates into the debate concerning unwantedness. If the baby dies inside the mother's womb, then it was an unviable fetus; but if that same fetus survives the abortion attempt and is delivered from the womb alive, it may well be viable but is still unwanted—and thereby still worthy of death. So far, a death inflicted in this way is not, according to the law, murder. The viability argument, then, seems to be only a thinly veiled version of the wantedness argument.

The "Wantedness" Argument

Every child, the pro-abortionists claim, should be a wanted child. A doctor states the pro-abortionist position in the article excerpted earlier: "There are many medical disorders that make the lives of their victims so unpleasant that abortion is a preferable alternative," she writes. She goes on to name Down's syndrome, the well-known "mongoloid" condition, as an affliction "for which abortions are performed," failing to mention the fact that Down's syndrome children are perhaps the most loving and lovable handicapped children in the world, with only diminished intelligence and unusual physical features as handicaps. The doctor hastens to detail the rare Tay-Sachs disease and Lesch-Nyhan (self-mutilating) syndrome, making her case for abortion on the basis of these uncommon cases.

She adds:

> Many of us who favor the availability of abortion do so because we hold very dear another right that is often neglected in this country: the right of every child to a stable home with loving parents. No child should be raised by a mother who would have aborted him had she been able. Parenthood is one of life's greatest joys, but it is also one of the most awesome responsibilities anyone can assume. It is far too sacred to be used as punishment for sexual indiscretion, for having been the victim of rape or for having parents who oppose sex education. Yet the reality is that most infants born to mothers who did not wish to be pregnant will nonetheless go home with them.
>
> Adoption cannot be the only answer, even if the mothers were willing, for if all the aborted fetuses were instead delivered at term and relinquished to adoption agencies, there would not be enough homes for them. Those who oppose public funding to assist poor women who desire abortions would do well to consider the expense of public support of unwanted children until they reach adulthood. . . .
>
> To those who assert that abortions may be sacrificing potential Beethovens or Michelangelos, I say that it is much more likely that we are sparing ourselves future Hitlers or Charles Mansons.

The argument is, at its root, demonic. It is ironic that the doctor suggests that such liberal abortions would prevent future Hitlers, since Hitler would heartily approve her murderous and elitist line of logic. After all, how did he justify the slaughter of millions of Jews? The issue then was also one of "wantedness."

In all of these semantic arguments, there is an over-arching debate. The war of words can be summarized as that between the "quality of life" ethic versus the "sanctity of life" ethic.

The "quality of life" ethic is self-centered, secularistic—with man playing God. The fruit of this is seen in our playing with words to rationalize the most heinous and damning sins. We are using semantics to support our commitment to becoming an idolatrous, immoral, murderous society. If unchecked, it will only lead to ruin.

"Abortion continues in our country because the abortionists have used euphemisms and untenable arguments to try to deny that abortion is killing preborn human beings and the shedding of innocent blood," as Nellie Gray, president of the March For Life in Washington, D.C., correctly summarizes the situation. "They have been successful in gaining support from doctors, lawyers, politicians, clergy, judges, government officials, health services, professional organizations—and of course the press and media. With this type of support abortionists are selling crime as a virtue, killing as a 'service,' crushing preborn babies as 'therapy,' and shedding the innocent blood of preborn children as women's liberation."

On the other hand, the "sanctity of life" ethic is the commitment of the Scriptures.

The Bible Argument

Biblically, the issue of abortion *is the shedding of innocent blood*. This is a primary concern of the

Scriptures, and on this the Word of God leaves no doubt as to its position.

Such issues as pro-choice, right of a woman to her own body, viability, wantedness, etc., are man-made arenas of discussion. Each of these issues has been conceived in our culture's God-ignoring, humanistic mindset—and then presented to us as if they were the proper points for the public debate. Let us deeply realize that these issues were not birthed from the Scriptures by those who revere the Word of God and who are committed to a "sanctity of life" ethic. No, they were invented pure and simple by those who espouse secularism, by those whose underlying ethic is the utilitarian "quality of life."

The appalling tragedy is that God-fearing people have naively accepted these issues as the correct ones—and willingly debated them as if they had merit. They have left unchallenged the basic humanistic birth of these issues. And so we have had the curious sight of pro-life people running to the Scriptures to see what it has to say about pro-choice, viability, wantedness, rights, etc. as if they were legitimate biblical issues, without any question as to their secular source. And, even more importantly, hardly raising even a suggestion that the issue biblically really might be something infinitely more basic and vital than these humanistic concerns. It is a great understatement to say that this blind error has been a blunder of horrendous proportions!

No, the fundamental biblical issue in abortion is the shedding of innocent blood. And it is time for God-fearing people of all religious backgrounds to call the debate exclusively to that—and insist it stay there!

As to "pro-choice," the Scriptures would condemn this sophistry which attempts to remain neutral to the shedding of innocent blood. The Scriptures would emphasize that the choice is to protect innocent life.

As to the right of a woman to her own body, the Word of God would emphasize that we are created in the image of God and that our life—our bodies—are gifts from Him. Our first consideration is not our rights; it is the responsible use and behavior of our bodies. Such a responsibility is first concerned that our bodies bring glory to God. It's a responsibility, for instance, that concerns itself with wholesome and beautiful attitudes toward sexual love. It accepts responsibility for God-given sexuality and fertility. This responsibility is not only a woman's, but a man's.

As to viability, the Scriptures would emphasize no such arbitrary designation, but would consider human life precious in all instances. We have been given a great creative gift. God is aware of each life at the moment of conception and even before. For instance, Christ's Incarnation was a pre-known fact—what if the Virgin Mary, pregnant and unwed, had decided for abortion? God told Jeremiah that He had known him before he was even formed in the womb. What about the promises to the parents of Isaac, Samson, Samuel or John the Baptist?

But really the question of viability, and all these questions, touches on an immeasurably larger question: *What value does our society place on human life?* Terrence Scanlon, in a review[11] of President Reagan's book, *Abortion and the Conscience of the Nation*, observed that "Reagan cut right through all the rhetorical underbrush around the question of abortion when he said, 'The real question today is not when human life begins, but, *What is the value of human life?*' " Biblically, that is the all-embracing question.

As to wantedness, the Bible makes clear that all children, regardless of their physical or mental condition, are loved by God and should be cherished and nurtured by the community. And with President Reagan we can add that with the many thousands of couples who desire to adopt children today, every child certainly can be wanted.

The bottom line? None of these issues—pro-choice, rights, viability, wantedness—are legitimate issues. They are modern diversions—and even anti-abortionists have tragically become caught up in them, trying to argue their own side and win.

The real issue is not pro-choice, not rights, not viability, not wantedness.

The real issue—biblically—*is the shedding of innocent blood,* something the Bible is not silent on.

The Bible is clear concerning the absolute protection that is to be afforded to the innocent human life. An unborn child is human life, and certainly an innocent human life.

We are familiar with those first two words of The Lord's Prayer: "Our Father," speaking of God. Being a father means there has been the begetting of new life, paternity, reproduction, conception. Our heavenly Father, who cares even for sparrows and lilies and grass, cares deeply for all human life, and especially that which is helpless and innocent.

The unborn child is the most helpless of the helpless, the most innocent of the innocent. Deep within the womb the Father views each one. The Giver of Life knows that the little one is growing and developing according to a precise genetic pattern that marvelously sprang into being at the moment of conception. And all that is being added basically is food and nurture. The Father sees the unborn child moving, playing, sucking its thumb . . . *and crying.*

The womb is now becoming the tomb.

Dr. Bernard Nathanson has made a graphic ultrasound recording of an actual abortion, and has placed it on videotape. The film is of an abortion technique performed during the first three months of pregnancy and vividly shows that the unborn die in agony.

In the video, the baby is shown at play in the womb. Then the suction instrument enters. The baby tries to move away, futilely, as the instrument nears. However, the suction probe finds its victim and in an instant tears off its head, crushes the skull and dismembers the body.

But just before this occurs there is a gripping scene, as Dr. Nathanson describes it: "The tape shows the child pulling away from the device with a *silent scream on its face,* only moments before it died."

A "silent scream . . ."

The blood of millions of aborted children cries to God, the heavenly Father, from physicians' clinics and hospital rooms for vengeance. And there is only one ear that really hears their silent scream—and each of those cries is loud to Him.

The number of cries keeps growing in the United States alone, at an average of one every twenty seconds, three a minute, some 4,200 a day, and a million and a half a year—and millions more worldwide. The number is no longer just growing, but rather exploding—with no end in sight.

Abortion kills helpless, innocent life by the official sanction of the state and society—murder, sanctioned and encouraged. Daily, in doctors' offices and abortion clinics around the country and world, thousands of women are told that they should abort their children. Society tells them it is right, normal, and moral for them to kill the innocent human life developing helplessly in their wombs.

And they do it.

America's hands, and those of the nations of the world, are covered with innocent blood. That innocent blood cries to God for vengeance.

The heavenly Father hears the silent cry of the innocents.

It is reaching a thunderous crescendo. And He will answer in judgment—just as He did with Israel and Judah.

Notes for Chapter Six

[1] *Informaton Please Almanac 1983*, A & W Publishers, p. 790.

[2] John Powell, S.J., *Abortion: The Silent Holocaust*, Argus Communications, 1981, p. 50.

[3] Ibid., p. 12.

[4] R.C. Sproul, *Ethics and the Christian*, Tyndale, 1983, pp. 85-86.

[5] Kevin Perrotta, "Leadership Groups Reject Christian Morality," *Pastoral Renewal*, October 1983, p. 24.

[6] Dr. Cynthia B. Cristofani in *Oregonian*, September 17, 1982.

[7] Ibid.

[8] Sproul, op. cit., p. 86.

[9] Ibid., pp. 86-87.

[10] Franky Schaeffer, *A Time for Anger*, Crossways Books, 1982.

[11] *Human Events*, October 1984.

CRY OF THE INNOCENTS

For He who avenges blood remembers;
He does not ignore the cry of the afflicted.
—Psalm 9:12 NIV

In spite of Israel's awful sins, in spite of America's terrible disregard for God's law, in spite of the crimes of any age in history, God's love still stretches, further and further—desperately far—holding back the crushing blows of judgment.

Not that mankind deserves mercy. In every age, God has made His law clear, and man has sloughed it off, embracing one form of idolatry or another. Leviticus 18:21 declares, "Do not give any of your children to be sacrificed to Molech, for you must not profane the name of your God" (NIV), yet the Israelites did exactly that.

God made the penalties clear, yet they were ignored. "Any Israelite or any alien living in Israel who gives any of his children to Molech must be put to death," God told Moses. "The people of the community are to stone him. I will set my face against that man and I will cut him off from his people; for by giving his children to Molech, he has defiled my sanctuary and profaned my holy name" (Lev. 20:1-3 NIV).

God even went a step further, detailing the penalties for ignoring those punishments: "If the people of the community close their eyes when that man gives one of his children to Molech and they fail to put him to death, I will set my face against that man and his family and will cut off from their people both him and all who follow him in prostituting themselves to Molech" (Lev. 20:4, 5 NIV).

But in spite of all this, God extends His grace to a sinful mankind. He waits. He withholds judgment. He loves.

It is because He is a caring God, not inclined to judgment, but inclined to mercy. He longs for His people to be reconciled to Him.

Still, after intolerable crimes, judgment does come. Closest to God's heart are the innocent ones, and when the twin sins of immorality and murder strike at the life of the innocent, God's judgment is sure.

"Do not put an innocent . . . to death," the Law states in Exodus 23:7, "for I will not acquit the guilty."

What is clearly stated here is that, while murder is wrong generally, the murder of an *innocent* victim is *especially* wrong, as we have seen.

Indeed, sins against the innocent are called "crying sins" in the Scriptures. God's Word refers to the innocent victim's blood "crying from the ground," appealing to God for His justice and retribution on the guilty. This is not fantasy, but a sound scriptural concept. In essence, what it means is that God takes the side of the guiltless or innocent victim.

And because God cares so deeply about the innocent, the blood of a single innocent cries from the ground—and God responds.

The Law was given for the protection of individuals—a sin does not have to be committed by an entire society before judgment comes. It was the single act of killing

Abel that brought judgment to Cain. It was the single act of killing the innocent Naboth that brought judgment on the greedy King Ahab and his evil Queen Jezebel at the place called Jezreel. The blood of a single innocent cries to God from the ground—and God has declared in His Word that He will hear that cry. And He does hear.

This concept goes back to the very beginning. When God confronted Cain concerning the whereabouts of his brother Abel, Cain denied he knew where his brother was. "The Lord said, 'What have you done? Listen! Your brother's blood cries out to me from the ground. Now you are under a curse and driven from the ground, which opened its mouth to receive your brother's blood from your hand'" (Gen. 4:10 NIV).

John J. Davis, commenting on these verses in his book *Paradise to Prison: Studies in Genesis,* says, "Cain, like most murderers, thought he had successfully concealed his deed. He had overlooked, however, the voice of his brother's blood, which cried out for judgment and justice. God had created life and could not tolerate the indiscriminate, unjustified slaughter of a man."[1]

The Arabs have a saying that the dew of heaven will not descend on a spot watered with innocent blood. A similar thought is conveyed in Isaiah 26:21:

> See, the Lord is coming out of his dwelling
> to punish the people of the earth for their sins.
> The earth will disclose the blood shed upon her;
> she will conceal her slain no longer.

Even Job cried to God, appealing to this concept of innocent blood being avenged: "O earth, do not cover my blood; may my cry never be laid to rest!" (Job 16:18 NIV).

Simply, the Old Testament teaches that every murder, however secret, will be brought to light: every murderer, however unsuspected previously, will be denounced and punished; and every innocent victim will be avenged by God personally. Each individual is that important to God—each individual is of immense, eternal worth.

The thought of God as Judge and Punisher is horrifying to many modern people. They have been deceived by well-intentioned teachers who do not fully understand God's character. God is sovereign in His divine judgment against man. We read in the *Theological Wordbook of the Old Testament*, Volume 2,

> God cannot be true to his character of holiness and justice if he allows sins and rebellion to go unpunished. The prophets stressed "the day of the Lord's vengeance" (Isa. 38:8, 62:2; 63:4) as times in history when the Lord sets the record straight. . . .
>
> God's vengeance must never be viewed apart from his purpose to show mercy. He is not *only* the God of wrath, but must be the God of wrath in order for his mercy to have meaning. . . .
>
> As the covenant God, he punishes those who break covenant with him. "I will smite you seven times, even I for your sins. And I will bring a sword upon you, that shall execute the vengeance of the covenant" (Lev. 26:24, 25).[2]

Thus, the Bible clearly establishes that God will punish the ultimate or "crying" sin against innocent life; that this is a sin upon which His vengeance and wrath is fully justified, since He is a holy and just God.

But Israel—and now America and much of Europe—went the next step as well. Not only did they murder innocents, but they made it part of their official agenda. Anderson and Freedman, in their commentary *Hosea*, state:

> The term *damin* [used in Hosea 4:2, "blood-shed follows bloodshed"] . . . refers to the shedding of innocent blood by official action, and the crime charged against the nation here, as elsewhere, is the formal sacrifice of human beings, in particular children who are *innocent* and unblemished, so as to meet sacrificial requirements. . . . The shedding of *innocent* blood (cf. Psalm 106:38) *is an ultimate crime* in the eyes of the great pre-exilic prophets, all of whom use the same or similar language; it symbolizes the ultimate rebellion against God in the destruction of human beings who are made in his image and represent him on earth. . . . This phrase relates specifically to the ritual sacrifice of human beings, especially children, and hence involves both leadership and people in a common and universal guilt.[3]

The relationship of Israel's child sacrifices to modern surgical abortion is clear. But to suggest the Bible does not speak to the abortion issue is mistaken. Gleason L. Archer, in his *Encyclopedia of Bible Difficulties*, gives this analysis of the issue of abortion from a biblical perspective:

> Psalm 139:13 indicates very definitely that God's personal regard for the embryo begins from the time of its inception. The psalmist says, "For Thou didst form my inward parts; Thou didst weave me in my mother's

womb" (NASB). Verse 16 continues: "Thine eyes have seen my unformed substance; and in Thy book they were all written, the days that were ordained for me, when as yet there was not one of them" (NASB). . . . Even though many thousands of embryos and fetuses are deliberately aborted every year throughout the world, *God cares about the unborn and takes personal knowledge of them just as truly before they are born as after their delivery.* He has their genetic code all worked out and has a definite plan for their lives (according to v. 16).

In Jeremiah 1:5 the Lord says to the young prophet on the threshold of his career, "Before I formed you in the womb I knew you, and before you were born I consecrated you; I have appointed you a prophet to the nations" (NASB). This certainly implies that God foreknew this lad even before he was conceived in his mother's womb. Apparently we human beings have an identity in God's mind that is established "from everlasting" —long before conception as an embryo. Second, the verse teaches that it is God Himself who forms that fetus and governs and controls all those "natural" processes that bring about the miracle of human life. Third, God has a definite plan and purpose for our lives, and each of us really matters to Him. Therefore anyone who takes the life of any human being at any stage in his life's career will have to reckon with God. "Whoever sheds man's blood, by man his blood shall be shed, for in the image of God He made man" (Gen. 9:6 NASB). When does an embryo begin to be a creature made in the image of God? From the moment of conception in the womb, Scripture says. Therefore God will require his blood at the hands of his murderer, whether the abortionist be a medical doctor or a nonprofessional.[4]

Archer goes on to point out, using detailed analysis of original Scripture texts, that God never assigns second-class status to the embryo or fetus, but always treats harm to the unborn child with at least as much care as any other life.[5]

This truth has been recognized for centuries. Tertullian, in his *Apologeticus* of A.D. 197, eloquently presents the case:

> For us murder is once for all forbidden; so even the child in the womb, while yet the mother's blood is still being drawn on to form the human being, it is not lawful for us to destroy. To forbid birth is only quicker murder. It makes no difference whether one take away the life once born or destroy it as it comes to birth. He is a man, who is to be a man; the fruit is always present in the seed.

Yet every year some *one and a half million* legal abortions are performed in the United States. According to a report by the Alan Guttmacher Institute in New York, and reported in *Evangelical Newsletter,* of those abortions in one year, 460,000 (or thirty percent) were aborted by primarily "young, white, and unmarried" women. Also, "Thirty percent were under age 30 and 1 percent under 15, 70 percent were white, 79 percent were unmarried, 58 percent were childless, and 67 percent had no previous abortions."

Harold O.J. Brown states the case thus:

> What brought on this dramatic change, from abortion as a last resort, to abortion as a widely

used convenience? Many factors coincided. From a spiritual perspective, no doubt the result of the refusal of so many Americans to honor God, or to be thankful, caused Him to give them over to a depraved mind and let them fall into patterns of thinking and acting that they themselves would have found horrifying not many years ago (Rom. 1:21, 28). From a sociological perspective, it is doubtless the consequence of the triumph of sexual permissiveness, of the "Playboy philosophy," of the growing acceptability of always putting self and self's desires first, heedless of the consequences to others. But from a legal perspective, it was one dramatic event, the 1973 decision of the United States Supreme Court, *Roe vs. Wade,* that took abortion out of the status of a despicable crime and made it an "acceptable medical procedure," part of the "full range of medical services."

. . . Although the Bible teaches that all sin is lawlessness and separates us from God, certain sins are especially condemned as so-called "crying sins." They injure the weak and helpless, who "have no avenger" on earth and who therefore cry out to God for justice. . . .

If we take Scripture seriously, we recognize that when society tolerates—not to say encourages and subsidizes—such crying sins, not only those who commit them will suffer. God will hold the whole land accountable. Indeed, it is possible to see a relationship between the reverses and defeats our country has suffered since 1973—the oil embargo, defeat and humiliation in Vietnam, rampant inflation, humiliation in Iran, and now inability to end a crippling economic recession and the Supreme Court's decision to make a "crying sin" into acceptable, recommended national practice. . . .

The "crying sin" of killing 1.5 million developing children every year will go on unpunished—until God visits His judgment on people who permit such sin when it is in their power to change it.[6]

It is, then, only by the grace of God that America has gone unpunished for its attitude toward abortion. This is why the church today plays such a crucial role—as did the prophets in Hosea's day.

God's special care for the innocents must be proclaimed, so that Americans can once again grasp the infinite value of each unborn child—and cease striking at God's gift of creation—and avoid cataclysmic doom!

THE CRY OF THE CHILDREN

A cry has gone out to the sons of men,
a cry from the throne of God,
what have you done with my little ones,
where have they gone.

I hear the cry of a child,
the cry of a million children,
I created the beauty on their faces,
now all I see is pain.

Come up here you men and women,
what is that on your hands,
the colour of crimson,
you spread death throughout the land.

You have taken the right to live
out of my hands,
do you realise what you've done,
many a child of blessing has never seen the sun.

Yes, they live with me; they will live forevermore,
and before you they shall stand,
on the day of judgement,
to condemn you, sinful man.

So arise you who would repent of this sin,
and I'll forgive you if you will turn aside,
for the cry of the children has come to my ears
and my face from them I will not hide.

© Therese Goodwin 1984[7]

Notes for Chapter Seven

[1] John J. Davis, *Paradise to Prison: Studies in Genesis*, Baker, 1975, p. 9.

[2] *Theological Wordbook of the Old Testament, Volume Two*, Moody Press, 1980. pp. 598-599.

[3] Anderson & Freedman, *Hosea*, Doubleday, 1980, pp. 338-339.

[4] Gleason L. Archer, *Encyclopedia of Bible Difficulties*, Zondervan, 1982, pp. 246-247.

[5] Ibid., pp. 247-248.

[6] Harold O.J., Brown, "Judgment Without Justice," *Fundamentalist Journal*, January 1983.

[7] P.O. Box 5042, Hastings, New Zealand.

A CULTURE POISONED

> Cholera is a judgment on dirty living,
> not because God arbitrarily favors clean people
> but because of the structure of that element of
> the universe. Flood and famine are judgments
> on the avarice that causes people to destroy
> forests for the sake of short-term profit. Such
> human activities are not wrong because they do
> not pay. They do not pay because they are
> wrong.
> —Herbert Schlossberg, *Idols for Destruction*

How insensitive can a society become? Is it possible
that a culture can become calloused to great evils, such
as immorality and murder? How far will any of us
rationalize?

Dr. James M. Boice, chairman of the International
Council on Biblical Inerrancy, tells an almost unbelievable
but true story. Between 1960 and 1963, it seems, ordinary
law-abiding citizens of the Connecticut city of New Haven
tried to execute innocent victims simply because a man
in a white coat told them to. They could hear the victim cry
in pain, and they knew they were responsible for his

suffering. In some situations, the victim was right next to them, pleading for mercy. But they continued to administer an electric shock strong enough to kill him.

That horrible true story came out of a Stanley Milgram study on obedience and authority. Milgram wanted to find out how the average, normal citizens of Nazi Germany could have allowed the execution of millions of innocents. Milgram's theory was that Americans would have acted differently. He set up an experiment to find out.

In a laboratory, a researcher in a white coat told volunteers that they would be participating in "learning exercises." Each volunteer was given the title of "teacher" and told to question another volunteer, who was given the title of "victim." For each wrong answer by the victim, the teacher was to administer an electric shock. For each additional wrong answer, the teacher was to increase the level of the shock, moving up the scale from mild to deadly.

There were thirty questions, Boice recalls, and thirty levels of shock. Thus, the "teacher" had to make up to thirty distinct decisions to shock the other person.

The "victims," however, were not actually receiving the shocks. They were merely acting. But the "teachers" did not know that. They thought they were actually inflicting torturous pain on their victims. And they continued to do it.

"Why did they continue to shock and finally 'kill' another human being," Boice asks, "against whom they had neither malice nor fear? The research was explicit, the answer horribly clear. They did it because a man in a white coat, whom they had never met before but who had the aura of authority, told them to do it. Thus, the ordinary citizens of New Haven were no different than the German soldiers who rounded up Jews." God was not the highest authority.

America's lax attitude toward abortion is a symptom of the larger sickness. Everywhere we look, there are evidences of Satan's tampering. His vile touch has left its mark on us all. We are all victims of the Fall, when Adam and Eve failed to resist Satan's temptation. And by ignoring God's directives and guidelines, as did the Israelites, we are just as subject to God's judgment for our failures. We have intentionally, as a country and a society, turned away from a God-centered way of life.

The twin sins are evident in our culture. Look at television and the movies. Where is God's hand in the programing and entertainment? Sexual promiscuity, homosexuality, adultery, and all of God's prohibitions are flaunted and touted as socially acceptable on television and in films. Violence plays an important part in these media, violence bred of an existential mindset, another tentacle of secular humanism.

What we see on our televisions and at the theaters are the reflections of those executives and artists in control of the majority of the visual media. It is a reflection of their anti-God, secular worldview, a view that holds that there is no God and no absolutes—only the self.

Evangelical Newsletter published the results of a poll taken among TV's producers and writers. The interviewers talked to 104 executives, producers, and writers representing "the cream of televisions's creative community." Some 93 percent had a religious upbringing; slightly more than half claimed any current religious affiliation. Barely 7 percent were regular churchgoers. Politically, the study showed the elite of the TV industry are "overwhelmingly" liberal.

Regarding abortion, 97 percent subscribed to the

"rights" argument—that a woman has the right to decide for herself whether or not to have an abortion. Four fifths disagreed that homosexuality is wrong. Only half felt *adultery* is wrong! Nearly 20 percent felt "strongly" that adultery is *not* wrong.

And, frighteningly, two thirds said TV's role should be to "promote social reform." Only 12 percent believed television to be "too critical of traditional values."

Obviously, these attitudes show through in the programing that is placed on the tube. Not only is their secularist viewpoint a matter of personal conviction, *it is also a matter of social activism.* Whatever means is available to them to promote their ideology, they will take advantage of it. Yet it's ironic that Christians who attempt to promote godly values through the media are harshly criticized for *proselytizing,* and forcing their "old-fashioned views" on others. *The question is: Who's forcing what on whom?*

It isn't only through the media that society's values are being challenged and continually changed according to the godless whims of the secular humanists. Their influence reaches into the classroom. In a detailed article which appeared in *Christianity Today*, Addie Jurs graphically describes a typical sex-education course given in public schools and sponsored and developed by Planned Parenthood. In the first half of the article, we are taken into the classroom through the eyes of two fictional sixteen-year-olds, Christy and John, and we vividly see what they are confronted with in their classroom.

One of the first things Christy encounters in the sex-education program is a film called *About Sex*.

The movie opened with a rock group singing, "Let's get together—sex. That's what it's all about—sex." A series of flashing pictures included a nude go-go dancer. Christy couldn't believe what she'd seen, and she was very attentive. She was particularly interested in what was said about premarital intercourse: "When a man and woman decide to have sex they should also decide if they want a baby." A Planned Parenthood clinic was shown as a helpful source of information and assistance.

As the film ended, Christy was puzzled. No one had mentioned marriage; masturbation was encouraged; homosexuality was presented as an acceptable option; and having an abortion sounded like a positive experience. Christy felt puzzled—had she missed something? The principles her parents had taught about the importance of marriage and the gift of children were never mentioned.

As the weeks passed and the course continued, their instructor "stressed the importance of being responsible" (using birth control to prevent pregnancy), and not judging other people's sexual choices. The students were asked to take positions on a variety of questions, and to do so before the class. No anonymity was allowed, and the options presented excluded biblically based options.

One day the class divided into small groups and were asked to share and write down all the slang terms they knew for penis, vagina, homosexual, and intercourse. This exercise was done in groups of mixed gender.

Christy and John were dating, and as they experienced the sex-education class together, they began to consider what it would mean for them to have sex. John cited their instructor, who had told them, "If you're ready and responsible, there's nothing wrong with having sex!" But Christy was still confused, and continued to search for more information. She read books her instructor recommended. One reference was *Our Bodies, Our Selves.* In it, loss of virginity was "viewed as a move from childhood to adulthood."

Christy also picked up some Planned Parenthood pamphlets. One, entitled, "So You Don't Want to Be a Sex Object," stated, "Accept sex for what it is, for whatever pleasure it gives you." Further, it described saving sex until marriage as the "old mythology," claiming those that held that view were "old-fashioned."

Following this graphic description of Christy's dilemma, the article goes on to describe the history and philosophy behind Planned Parenthood, and the incredible influence the organization has. The article is shocking in its revelations concerning the activities of Planned Parenthood. But what is even more revealing is the fact that Planned Parenthood, while a private organization, receives heavy federal funding and support *Its activities are sanctioned by the state!*

Father Paul Marx, a Catholic priest and head of Human Life International headquartered in Washington, D.C. says of Planned Parenthood:

> I know of no worldwide organization more dangerous to Church and mankind, more destructive to youth, family and religion . . . For more than thirty years I have tracked PP.

He adds this evaluation:

> "Planned Parenthood" is a devilishly subtle euphemism and misnomer. Whatever PP

plans it is not the family. In their literature and in their meetings they speak not of spouses, but of "sexual partners"; they use the term "sexually active" when they mean fornication and adultery. While parroting the slogans "freedom of choice" and "reproductive freedom," they deceive many who have no knowledge of authentic freedom. By "sexual freedom" PP means intercourse with anybody —just so there is mutual consent and contraceptive precaution to avoid that tragedy of tragedies, an unwanted child. If a child is conceived, they suggest abortion: "the second line of defense against the unwanted child," or, "post-conceptive family planning." . . . Perhaps a more accurate name for PP would be "Planned Barrenhood" or "Banned Parenthood."

Planned Parenthood, seemingly, was once an organization with a somewhat different orientation toward abortion. A 1963 pamphlet stated, "An abortion kills the life of a baby after it has begun. It is dangerous to your life and health. It may make you sterile so that when you want a child you cannot have it.")

All of this anti-biblical influence is having a devastating effect on the family. In 1960, there were 1,523,000 recorded marriages and 393,000 divorces. In 1981, the figures jumped: 2,438,000 marriages and 1,219,000 divorces. This information is listed in the *Information Please Almanac*, which also includes the following statement beneath its divorce/marriage statistics chart:

Children of divorce constitute one of the fastest growing segments of the American population. Since 1972 more than a million additional children annually have had their homes disrupted by divorce. One third of the nation's children will undergo this experience by the time they are 18, according to a widely used estimate.[2]

This corresponds to the dramatic increase of one-parent homes and those who simply choose to remain unmarried. More than twenty percent of all American households in 1982 were one-person households. And homes of six or more individuals had dropped to just over five percent—down from 10.6 percent in 1970.

One out of every eight children lives in a single-parent home. For every thousand married people, there are 109 divorced people. Almost two million households are made up of men and women living together outside marriage. Births out of wedlock jumped thirty-five percent between 1960 and 1970. From 1970 to 1982, the number of people living alone increased by seventy-five percent, resulting from what has been termed "American commitment to self-determination." In other words, it is a result of purely selfish motives.

It is this total disruption of the family and the flourishing of promiscuous "liberated" sex, combined with self-centered determinism, that has resulted in the dramatic increase in abortion. Also, another tragic result of all this self-serving freedom has been a near epidemic of venereal disease, and the appearance of a new, incurable strain—herpes II. In fact, herpes II is so widespread that even those who have touted "free sex" for years are beginning to reexamine their positions—and even to call for a return to monogamous relationships. This phenomenon is becoming even more noticeable with the rise of such "new" diseases as AIDS.

However positive this new twist may be, the motives are essentially wrong. Fear of disease is not the proper motivation for sexual faithfulness, especially when science will very probably come up with a cure eventually. When a cure does arise, the call for "free sex" will again be sounded. In fact, already, those who suffer from herpes but advocate and desire sexual promiscuity are claiming that herpes II can be controlled and is not as dangerous as many have claimed.

While herpes II and AIDS are serious diseases, they usually involve victims who willingly chose to engage in illicit sexual activity.

A much worse disease is the cancerous spreading of abortion on demand. The victims of abortion have no say in the matter.

Every year in America some 1.5 million abortions are reported. Of these, one third are performed on teenagers. And each year the statistic grows. The increase in abortion is directly related to the decline in morality in other areas. As sexual license increases, so do abortions.

An item in *Christianity Today* as long ago as January 31, 1969, states, "The Western world is coming alarmingly close to the establishment of sex worship. And the closer we come to the sex practices of ancient, pagan cultures, *the closer we come to sharing their oblivion*" (italics mine).

Sexual license decreases the value of human life. Instead of individuals being seen as unique and precious, persons become significant only in relation to the amount of pleasure that can be derived from them. Whether this pleasure is intellectual, emotional, or physical, the principle is the same.

Pornography, in all its forms, highlights the pleasure principle. Men and women are portrayed merely as objects of pleasure. Sex is sought after as the ultimate "high."

The more one has, the better. The tragedy is that, the more one immerses himself, the more debauched—and less satisfied—he becomes. And the less and less valuable human life becomes. Perversions thus flourish. One of those perversions is abortion.

Abortion has become a nearly casual consideration in today's society. In fact, for many women, to have an abortion is a symbol of prestige. It is the ultimate "statement" of one's right to one's own body. It is chic.

It requires an incredible state of mind to consider life so casually and to kill it. But it happens because it isn't cloaked in terms of killing or murder. Those involved in abortion aren't such "bad folk." "They are not spectacularly wicked souls, filled with divine madness," Susan Austin writes. "On the whole, as we all admit, they are perfectly ordinary and trying to be, if not good, at least acceptable. *They kill because no one calls it killing. . . .*

"In our collective body, to bear and rear children is now often considered trivial and even degrading work; it has become our custom to find our satisfaction outside the home, and we talk of being 'trapped' by our children."[3]

It is this thinking that leads to the further justification of killing the unborn because "every child should be a wanted child." While this sounds like a lovely statement, it is a subtly demonic concept.

The "wantedness" argument has infected our once honorable medical community. Just recently, a couple who were expecting twins were told that one of the babies suffered from Down's syndrome. The parents chose to abort that child. The doctors placed a needle through the mother's abdomen and into the unwanted baby's heart. Blood was drawn out of the heart, causing a fatal heart attack (and no doubt painful death) in the infant. At full term, the healthy, normal baby was delivered, followed by the shriveled corpse of the unwanted baby, who was discarded. Is this what God intended?

William Brennan, a professor in the School of Social Service at St. Louis University, correctly compares abortion and genetic tampering to practices that took place during the Nazi holocaust.

> Involvement of the German doctors in the Nazi holocaust represented the most radical departure from the ethics of the Hippocratic oath in the history of western civilization. . . .
>
> Today, only 35 plus years after the defeat of Naziism, doctors are again perpetrating a huge orgy of antiseptic, technically flawless, killing.[4]

An unwittingly perceptive reader gives us insight into the abortion mentality of our culture, with this response to a newspaper's pro-abortion editorial: "Let's be honest. Don't we feel threatened by deformed children? These children are the epitome of need. They require unselfish giving and that is beyond our comprehension. When society can put aside its self-centeredness, I will be against abortions. But when that time comes, I don't think there will be a need for them."

Children in need are no longer the object of every doctor's concern. They have become, instead, targets for extermination.

In spite of what is an obvious cruelty and outrage to many, abortions continue and the numbers increase annually. Also, abortions become easier and easier to obtain. Already, a husband can no longer stop his wife from having an abortion if she chooses.

And in most states, a teenager can obtain an abortion without her parents' consent—in spite of the fact that she would not be permitted to have her tonsils or appendix removed unless her parents were to sign consent forms!

"The fact that some of the most influential men and women in American society have embraced these values is very important," writes Kevin Perrotta, "simply because these people *are* influential. They are more than weathervanes showing which way the wind blows. They are the transmission belts of the social machinery, carrying the force of neopagan ideas into its every part." [5]

Satan has been very successful in perverting God's intent. God's plan has been completely twisted by secular society, His laws totally ignored. The result has been unrestricted sexual license, savage disruption of the family unit, an outbreak of sexual disease, complete perversion of sexual relationships, and wholesale murder of the most innocent of innocents—unborn babies. The twin sins are evident.

There is one small bright spot. In Stanley Milgram's study on obedience and authority, in which ordinary Connecticut citizens were persuaded by a man in a white coat to "kill" innocent victims, there did turn out to be a few rebels. Not everyone was obedient. One volunteer, a New England minister, gave three shocks out of thirty but then refused to administer any more.

"If one has as one's ultimate authority God," he said later, "then it trivializes human authority."

That minister had not forgotten the highest authority when confronted with an imposing human authority figure in a white lab coat.

Still, he was an exception.

The question we are confronted with now is: How does the world rationalize such wanton disregard for human life? How can such "nice people" become so completely caught up in this massive destruction of human life?

And exactly who will pay for the heinous murder of the innocents?

Notes for Chapter Eight

[1] Addie Jurs "Planned Parenthood Advocates Permissive Sex," *Christianity Today,* September 3, 1982.

[2] *Information Please Almanac 1983,* A & W Publishers.

[3] Susan Austin, "The Aborting Community," *Evangelical Newsletter,* January 7, 1983.

[4] William Brennan, "The Holocaust: Naziism and Abortion," *Fundamentalist Journal,* January 1983, p. 31.

[5] Kevin Perrotta, "Leadership Groups Reject Christian Morality," *Pastoral Renewal,* October 1983, p. 24.

LESSONS PAST

A nation that covenants with God at its inception, is not only singularly privileged; it is doubly accountable.
—Virginia Corfield
comparing Israel and America in *Sow the Wind*[1]

People fail to appreciate the worth of society's Christian underpinnings because they are unconscious recipients of its blessings. The most vigorous atheist in the West has grown up in a world in which love and justice are ideals.
—Herbert Schlossberg, *Idols for Destruction*

There is a familiar saying reminding us that those who do not learn from the lessons of history are doomed to repeat them. If this is true of secular history, it is even more so of biblical history. The insights gained from the living accounts of the Scriptures, about real people in real places facing real issues like those today, can give us critical guidance.

It was from such a perspective that Carl Henry spoke to our nation in his address to the 40th Annual National

Religious Broadcasters Convention. "What distinguishes the present moral decline in America from that of earlier generations? Simply this: today's secular *mindset* rests as never before upon a non-biblical *willset.*"

Henry then reflected on how throughout history the will of man has been set against the will of God. This brought him to observe that "pagan rebellion in ancient times actually escalated until God irrevocably 'gave them over' " (Rom. 1:24, 26, 28).

"The Creator responded to mankind's insistent and unyielding rejection of Him," Henry added, "by finally *abandoning rebellious humanity* to its own determinate intellectual depravity, degrading passions, and moral impurity. . . . Now the West is reverting to its pagan and pre-Christian readiness *to murder the innocents and the defenseless, to destroy unwanted infants, to dispose of the maimed and the elderly.*"

Malcolm Muggeridge too has taught lessons from history. Looking at more recent secular history, Muggeridge in 1977 made a chilling observation about his native England which has legalized abortion:

> There have been more deaths, as a result of our Abortion Act, than in the First World War. I was brought up to believe that one of the great troubles of the Western World was that in the First World War we lost the flower of our population. Well now we have destroyed an equivalent number of lives, in the name of humane principles, before they were even born. . . .
>
> Though in worldly terms the battle has been lost, and abortion is now legalized throughout Europe, and in the Western Hemisphere, *it still*

remains the most important issue confronting us, and . . . nothing can take away the importance of that issue.[2]

Muggeridge's incisive historical view moves to the future as well, to where he sees abortion propelling us toward euthanasia:

The fact is that because it's so costly in money and personnel to keep alive people about whom the medical opinion is that their lives are worthless, the temptation to get rid of the burden by killing them off will be even greater. . . . The only government so far in the history of the world to put euthanasia law into effect is the government of the Nazis . . . and to a considerable extent the German medical profession cooperated with them. . . . Before long euthanasia will be legalized like abortion, like Family Planning, because all these things are closely related. *They're all a slippery slope, one leading inexorably to the other.*[3]

The historical panorama expands as J. Randall Peterson looks at our day and back at biblical times. "We live in a sex-crazy age," he writes in *The Bible Newsletter*. "But so did . . . Hosea. . . . We are bombarded with sexual statistics, sexual images, sexual urges. But our world is really just one high-tech step away from the Canaanites. . . . *We can learn much from our predecessors.*"

Peterson explains:

The Canaanites made a religion out of sex. They had a father god and a mother god who created the world with their sexual union.

Various sexual rites were performed in the worship of these gods. "Sacred" prostitution was common. Into this context, Joshua led the children of Israel. They fared well in battle against the Canaanites, but when it came to settling in side-by-side with them, many Israelites fell prey to the Canaanites' "sex-as-religion" propaganda.

Then Peterson brings it home to our day: "Our current culture also seems to be making a religion out of sex. Sex is the answer, we are told again and again. . . . As far as today's Canaan is concerned, you *are* your sexuality."

"Canaan tells lies," says Fleming Rutledge of Grace Church in New York (quoted by Peterson), "very convincing and very seductive lies. . . . A system of lies not only deceives, but also destroys."

Reflecting on today's milieu, Herbert Schlossberg gives the very sharpest conclusion: "When Israel began worshiping the Canaanite gods, it was only a matter of time before *the nation began shedding innocent blood.*"[4]

Schlossberg points then to our own day:

> After biblical faith wanes, a people can maintain habits of thought and self-restraint. The ethic remains after the faith that bore it departs. But eventually a generation arises that no longer has the habit, and that is when the behavior changes radically.

And then he summarizes: "The generation now alive has remained true to many vestiges of the biblical faith. These remnants are the smile of the Cheshire cat, remaining for a time after the disappearance of the entity in which it was incarnated."

To the current religious world, Schlossberg issues a serious dictum: "Churches are no less subject to judgment than are other institutions, and they will learn this truth as did the faithless prophets who were contemporaries of Amos and Isaiah."[5]

All of these are sobering analyses of the lessons of the past. But the most instructive historical exercise comes from the scriptural record itself. Chronicled in the Old Testament are the parallel accounts of two Hebrew nations, both a part of the covenant people of God. They are Israel and Judah, and we have alluded to their accounts several times. Let us look deeper.

The division of the one nation into two separate countries goes back to the time just after the death of Solomon when there was a conflict over taxation. Rehoboam, Solomon's son on the throne, wouldn't listen to the entreaty of Jeroboam I, who spoke for many of the people in asking for an easing of the burden.

The result was that the nation divided, with Jeroboam leading the ten northern tribes in secession and forming a new government with the capital in Samaria.

From then on, that northern kingdom was called Israel and the southern kingdom Judah.

Both Israel and Judah shared a common heritage before God. After they divided, God sent each nation special prophets who spoke pointedly to each nation's spiritual and moral needs.

The interesting thing is that not only were Israel and Judah's heritages identical, but the spiritual problems they developed, their declines into idolatry and their eventual judgments by God were the same.

Both nations drifted from their spiritual moorings at about the same place; both took up the worship of false gods, intermingling it with the worship of God; both expressed their idolatry ultimately in gross immorality and murder of innocents; both were warned by prophets from God who called for repentance and renewal; both ignored the warnings; and as a result, both were judged by God by being overthrown and taken captive by heathen powers.

We can learn much—very much—from their stories.

Perhaps the most powerful—and sobering—lesson we can gain from these two nations is *how both Israel and Judah themselves did not learn the lessons of history.*

Caught up in their idolatrous lifestyles, paying lip service to God, ignoring His Law, rejecting the proclamations of the prophets—even killing some of them—rationalizing their actions, and divorcing themselves from predicted judgment, Israel and Judah plunged ahead, stubbornly putting aside in their thinking the lesson that history—their history—taught them: the sinful things they were doing had always brought tragic consequences until there was repentance.

One graphic example is pointed to by Jeremiah. This prophet speaks to Judah very pointedly:

> If you really change your ways and your actions and deal with each other justly, if you do not oppress the alien, the fatherless, or the widow *and do not shed innocent blood in this place,* and if you do not follow other gods to your own harm, then I will let you live in this place . . . *But look, you are trusting in deceptive words that are worthless* (Jer. 7:5-8 NIV, emphasis added).

What were these deceptive words they were trusting? "This is the temple of the Lord, the temple of the Lord, the temple of the Lord." They said it three times, to emphasize it most strongly. "We are safe—safe to do all these detestable things" (Jer. 7:4, 10 NIV).

Judah was self-deceived into thinking that because they had the temple they could do as they wished and God would not deal with them.

But God, through Jeremiah, gave them a history lesson. He recalled a place they knew well: Shiloh, "where I first made a dwelling for my Name."

At Shiloh God dwelt once also. And the people back at that time did wickedly. What did God do then? He removed His presence and judged the people.

The same would happen now: "Therefore, what I did to Shiloh I will now do to the house that bears my Name, the temple you trust in. . . . I will thrust you from my presence, just as I did all your brothers" (Jer. 7:14, 15 NIV).

Over and over again in his book, Jeremiah calls attention to Judah's idolatry, to their shedding of innocent blood. At the close of chapter seven, Jeremiah records God's words, which paint the vivid picture of idolatry once again:

> The people of Judah have done evil in my eyes, declares the Lord. They have set up their detestable idols in the house that bears my Name and have defiled it. They have built the high places of Topheth in the Valley of Ben Hinnom *to burn their sons and daughters in the fire.* . . . So beware, the days are coming, declares the Lord, when people will no longer call it Topheth or the Valley of Ben Hinnom, but the Valley of Slaughter (Jer. 7:30-32 NIV).

A very similar charge is laid in chapter nineteen:

For they have forsaken me and made this a place of foreign gods; they have burned sacrifices in it to gods . . . and they have filled this place with the blood of the innocent. They have built the high places of Baal to burn their sons in the fire (Jer. 19:4, 5 NIV).

And Jeremiah continues in chapter twenty-two: "This is what the Lord says: Do what is just and right. Rescue from the hand of his oppressor the one who has been robbed. Do no wrong or violence to the alien, the fatherless or the widow, and *do not shed innocent blood in this place.* . . . But your eyes and your heart are set only on dishonest gain, and *on shedding innocent blood* and on oppression and extortion" (Jer. 22:3, 17 NIV, emphasis added).

Jeremiah was a prophet for many years to Judah, continuing until the nation went into Babylonian captivity as he predicted over and again they would.

Perhaps the most flagrant example of ignoring the lesson of history was Judah's attitude during Jeremiah's ministry. Not only did Judah have the privilege of the ongoing perspective of Jeremiah's preaching, but they had the very, very real recent memory of their sister nation to the north, Israel, who had been overthrown and taken captive by the fierce Assyrians.

Such an event—the downfall of an entire nation—was no small thing. It was momentous. And it should have stood as vivid, living instruction, to Judah and the world, of the real consequences of sinful pursuits. It should have, but it didn't.

Israel's example was tragic. Hosea and Amos were raised up by God in Israel's closing years, the last writing prophets to the nation. Amos was the earlier of the two.

He came to Israel when the nation was politically and economically at its highest point. It was late in the forty-one-year reign of Jeroboam II, probably around 755 B.C.

Amos was an improbable prophet. His family had no prophetic background; he was a shepherd and a tender of sycamore trees; he wasn't even from Israel, but from Tekoa in Judah to the south.

But Amos had a message, a burning message, probably the sternest message of any prophet in the Old Testament. Except for the very end of his book, where there is a ray of hope, Amos preaches message after message of unrelenting denunciation against the sinning Israel, naming their iniquities in the most graphic manner.

But the improbable prophet preached his message of judgment in the most improbable atmosphere. There was certainly nothing in the nation's circumstances to suggest forthcoming doom. There was nothing to hint that in about three decades the nation would be completely devastated, that it would be no more.

No, the nation was enjoying material prosperity, business was growing. The people, at least those who enjoyed the fruit of prosperity, were self-sufficent. War was not a threat. The mood was complacent, secure.

But it was, in the words of Charles Dickens, "the best of times, the worst of times." For below the external successful image, there was eating at the nation's vitals the cancerous sin of forgetting God.

Irving Jensen describes it: "The rich were getting richer, and the poor were getting poorer. Idolatry, hypocrisy, moral corruption, and social injustices were everywhere. The nation was truly on the brink of disaster."[6]

The nation's sin, as Amos saw it, was *great insensitivity to the needs of others*. Such a sin, if not checked by repentance, always keeps producing social and legal evils.

In its clamor for free expression of all its varied forms of self-seeking, a society will cloak such sins in the very best clothes of respectability.

For instance, in our own American history, political and religious leaders were among the slaveholders who insisted they were right!

Today, such things as pornography, homosexual rights and abortion are openly promoted—insisted upon—as legal and honorable expressions of our society's highest conscience. In the forefront are leading men and women from law, politics, religion, and the entire gamut of public life.

It was this sin of insensitivity that Amos so fiercely inveighed against. Amos knew, as we have already seen, that unhalted insensitivity has had, in any society, only one ultimate terminus: *murder.*

Look again at Cain killing Abel. At Jezebel and Ahab killing Naboth. At the Romans killing the Christians. At America murdering her children. The path to such crimes is insensitivity, selfishness.

Judah should have learned from the Israel of Amos's day. America should learn from both.

A contemporary of Amos who apparently preached to Israel for a much longer period than Amos did was a man named Hosea. In fact, Hosea was the very last voice from God to the falling nation, according to the biblical record. He probably lived to see the Assyrian overthrow and watch his people marched off to captivity in 721 B.C.

Hosea and Jeremiah were much alike both in their message and in the deep, compassionate feeling with which they preached. Both had very, very difficult prophetic lives. They were called upon to stand in the most tragic times and warn their respective nations of impending judgment. But they did it courageously.

As we have seen, Hosea, after the opening account of his relationship with Gomer in chapters one through three, begins the message of his book in chapter four with a summary of Israel's sins.

It is legal language, the setting is a courtroom, and Hosea takes the part of the aggressive prosecuting attorney presenting to the jury the outline of his case, the charge from God against the nation.

Tersely he defines the problem: "There is no faithfulness, no love, no acknowledgment of God in the land" (Hos. 4:1 NIV).

Then he pinpoints the particular sins: "There is only cursing, lying and murder, stealing and adultery."

Quite a list. Quite a charge, which he goes on to amplify later in his book.

But then, to show the awful extent to which sin has plunged the defendant-nation, Hosea bursts forth with an overwhelming claim: "They break all bounds, and bloodshed follows bloodshed."

Biblical scholars tell us that Hosea is here calling attention to the crime of formal human sacrifice, in particular the sacrifice of "children who are innocent."

"The shedding of innocent blood is an ultimate crime," one scholar notes. "It symbolizes the ultimate rebellion against God in the destruction of human beings who are made in His image."

The phrase *bloodshed follows bloodshed* "relates specifically to the ritual sacrifice of human beings, especially children, and hence both leadership and people in a common and universal guilt."

That guilt would go unabated because the nation would remain unrepentant and continue in its idolatrous, immoral, and murderous path.

Hosea proclaimed the message of the Lord, but to an

unhearing nation, a nation absorbed in its sexual license—the "religion of sex" and its callous slaughter of innocents, all a part of its false worship, its religious apostasy.

The nation sank from its material prosperity during Jeroboam II's time. It degenerated steadily, economically as well as morally and spiritually. There were attempts to rise, but Israel was inextricably mired in the quicksand.

Finally, weakened, deteriorating, they faced the judgment of God. The Assyrians marched in and bloodily raped the once proud nation.

Judah should have learned from Israel's downfall. But did they?

On the throne of Judah at the time of Israel's fall was the God-fearing king Hezekiah. His reign was a good time for Judah. Hezekiah's reign was marked by an outstanding miracle of protection, when the Assyrians came against Jerusalem. Because Hezekiah and the people cried out to the Lord, the Angel of the Lord killed 185,000 Assyrian soldiers in one night. The Assyrian army was devastated and left Judah, returning to Nineveh.

It was a momentous miracle.

Hezekiah also led the nation in joyous revival. The thirtieth chapter of 2 Chronicles records that the country celebrated the Feast of Unleavened Bread so enthusiastically that after the required seven days they happily celebrated another seven!

But the bright days of Hezekiah would turn to the spiritual gloom of Manasseh, Hezekiah's son, who succeeded him on the throne.

Manasseh had two distinctions: he reigned longer than any other king in Jerusalem (fifty-five years), and he led the nation into the greatest idolatry and sin of its long history.

Although his reign had many marks of success, politcally and economically, his reign was a moral and spiritual disaster. The political and economic successes in the end made little difference. The moral and spiritual failures cost the nation its very life. Under Manasseh, Judah too took the ultimate steps toward judgment.

"Surely these things happened to Judah according to the Lord's command, in order to remove them from His presence *because of the sins of Manasseh,* and all he had done, including the *shedding of innocent blood.* For he had filled Jerusalem with *innocent blood,* and the Lord was not willing to forgive" (2 Kings 24:3, 4 NIV, emphasis added).

The account of Manasseh coming to the throne, according to both 2 Kings 21 and 2 Chronicles 33, is a tale of determined apostasy. Manasseh took the nation into every evil imaginable, and did so in a wholesale fashion: idolatry, desecration of the temple, sorcery, the occult, astrology, seances, the spilling of innocent blood, and more.

The Scripture record says that "Manasseh led them [Judah] astray, so that they did more evil than the nations the Lord had destroyed before the Israelites" (2 Kings 21:9 NIV).

The killing of innocents is particularly pinpointed later in the same chapter: "Moreover, Manasseh also shed so much innocent blood that he filled Jerusalem from end to end—besides the sin that he had caused Judah to commit, so that they did evil in the eyes of the Lord" (2 Kings 21:16).

Eventually Manasseh repented, but when he died, his son Amon came to the throne. He continued his father's evil practices. But Amon's reign was cut short after two years when he was assassinated by members of his own government.

This brought the youthful but God-fearing Josiah to head the nation. His thirty-one-year reign brought a ray of renewal, a glimmer of revival.

Some years into his tenure, Josiah ordered the neglected temple to be repaired. It was a worthy endeavor. But during the work, a most remarkable discovery was made, a find that would have a most profound impact on the nation: a copy of the Book of the Law was found.

The high priest gave it to Josiah's secretary to show the king. The secretary read from it to Josiah. As the king listened to the long-lost words of God, the effect on him was dramatic:

> When the king heard the words of the Book of the Law, he tore his robes. He gave these orders . . . Go and inquire of the Lord for me and for the people and for all Judah about what is written in this book . . . Great is the Lord's anger that burns against us because our fathers have not obeyed the words of this book (2 Kings 22:11-13 NIV).

Immediately Josiah acted to restore the nation to its original place before God. He did away with idolatry, got rid of the places for the shrine prostitutes, tore up the high places, put away every vestige of the previous spiritual degeneracy—including Topheth in the Valley of Ben Hinnom "so no one could use it to sacrifice his son or daughter in fire to Molech" (2 Kings 23:10 NIV).

Following this, Josiah reinstituted the worship of God by celebrating the Passover again. It was a great time in Judah.

The Scriptures say no king before or after turned to the Lord so completely as Josiah, "with all his heart and with all his soul and with all his strength, in accordance with all the Law of Moses."

However, the Bible adds a sobering word: "Nevertheless, the Lord did not turn away from the heat of his fierce anger, which burned against Judah because of all that Manasseh had done to provoke Him to anger" (2 Kings 23:26 NIV).

Although the nation seemed under Josiah to experience a genuine turnaround from the sins of Manasseh, their real heart was exposed after Josiah's untimely death in battle. After Josiah was gone, both the kings and the people plunged right back into their previous sin.

Judah didn't learn from the example of Israel, nor did they heed the preachings of Jeremiah. This great prophet proclaimed that Judah would go into Babylonian captivity for seventy years. The positive-preaching false prophets of his day rebuked Jeremiah for his message of judgment and wrongly promised the nation "peace, peace" instead.

Jeremiah held firm. But even with the hordes of Babylon outside the gates of Jerusalem in seige, Judah would not repent.

Finally, like Israel some 136 years before, Judah—deteriorated with the same culminating sins—fell to the Babylonians under the judgment of God, in 586 B.C.

Why didn't they listen? Why didn't they learn?

The fall of God's people is soberly and poignantly put in Psalm 106:34-41 (NIV):

> They did not destroy the peoples
> as the Lord had commanded them,
> But they mingled with the nations
> and adopted their customs.
> They worshiped their idols,
> which became a snare to them.
> They sacrificed their sons
> and their daughters to demons.

They shed innocent blood,
the blood of their sons and their daughters,
whom they sacrificed to the idols of Canaan,
and the land was desecrated by their blood.
They defiled themselves by what they did;
by their deeds they prostituted themselves.
Therefore the Lord was angry with His people
and abhorred His inheritance.
He handed them over to the nations,
and their foes ruled over them.

Judgment came. And the twin sins of murder and immorality are pinpointed as expressions of the great idolatry which brought the downfalls.

Later, Ezekiel would bring the message again, specifically bringing attention to the twin sins:

> The Lord said to me . . . Confront them
> with their detestable practices, for they have
> committed adultery and blood is on their
> hands. They committed adultery with their
> idols; they even sacrificed their children, whom
> they bore to me, as food for them. . . . On the
> very day they sacrificed their children to their
> idols, they entered my sanctuary and desecrated
> it (Ezek. 23:36-39 NIV).

Ezekiel also confirmed the judgment:

> But righteous men will sentence them to the
> punishment of women who commit adultery
> and shed blood, because they are adulterous
> and blood is on their hands. . . . So I poured
> out my wrath on them because they had shed
> blood in the land and because they had defiled

it with their idols. I dispersed them among the nations . . . I judged them according to their conduct and their actions (Ezek. 23:45; 36:18, 19 NIV).

With the graphic record of history, no wonder Carl Henry could aptly observe for us all that we in the West are "reverting to our pagan and prechristian readiness to murder the innocents and the defenseless."

What about our beloved America? Thomas Jefferson said, "I tremble for my country when I remember that God is just, and that His justice will not sleep forever."

In a certain sense America has already suffered judgment for the oppression of innocent human beings. Look at slavery and the Civil War.

Historians generally agree that there were many factors that contributed to the Civil War. Certainly slavery was a basic issue.

In that war nearly 530,000 men and women died, either from combat or disease. It had more American casualties than any other war the nation has ever fought in, more than World War I (116,500) and more than World War II (405,400). Plus there was the staggering financial cost of probably over $15 billion, and the devastation to the land.

The total amount of slaves this country had throughout its earlier years is probably unknown. However, it went into the thousands. We can only speculate how close that number of slaves comes to 530,000, the total number of men and women who died in our terrible, bloody Civil War.

Did we reap what we sowed?

Each year there are some one and one-half million abortions in America. This is more than all the men and women who had died in combat from the Revolutionary War to Vietnam. For human life, the womb is the single most dangerous place to be today. The moral equivalent today of the slavery issue is abortion, the shedding of innocent blood. It should give us pause.

Under God, we have been singularly blessed. Will we learn from history?

The jury is still out.

Notes for Chapter Nine

[1] Provident Press, 1979.

[2] Malcolm Muggeridge in *Evangelical Newsletter*, May 13, 1983.

[3] Ibid.

[4] Herbert Schlossberg, *Idols for Destruction*, Thomas Nelson, 1983, p. 296.

[5] Ibid.

[6] Irving Jensen, *Minor Prophets of Israel*, Moody Press, 175, p. 45.

GUILTY PARTY

After biblical faith wanes, a people can maintain habits of thought and of self-restraint. The ethic remains after the faith that bore it departs. But eventually a generation arises that no longer has the habit, and that is when the behavior changes radically. There is no protection against this in statutes or constitutions, which become scraps of paper when people come to despise the law that stands behind them. . . .

The generation now alive has remained true to many vestiges of the biblical faith. These remnants are the smile of the Cheshire cat, remaining for a time after the disappearance of the entity in which it was incarnated.

—Herbert Schlossberg, *Idols for Destruction*[1]

In his compelling play *The Visit* (which was later made into a classic film), Friedrich Duerrenmatt paints a vivid picture of the process whereby otherwise honest human beings rationalize themselves into deep hypocrisy. In the story, a small European town goes bankrupt, and the only person who can save the community is a very wealthy woman who once lived there. She is soon to return for a visit, and when she does, she agrees to restore the town's economic base. But there is a price: she wants the life of the town's foremost citizen. It seems that he got her pregnant when she was a girl, and deserted her.

At first the entire town is disgusted by the rich woman's proposal, but as the story continues, the various segments of the community—the justice system, the educational system, the business community, the town council, the church, and eventually even the man's own family—each one caves in. Each group somehow finds a way to rationalize away the value of one man's life in exchange for the common good.

There is no happy ending to Duerrenmatt's story. The man is murdered, the town is restored, and hypocrisy prevails.

"Rescue those being led away to death," Proverbs advises; "hold back those staggering toward slaughter. If you say, 'But we knew nothing about this,' does not he who weighs the heart perceive it? Does not he who guards your life know it? Will he not repay each person according to what he has done?" (Prov. 24:11-12 NIV).

The writer of the Proverbs asks chilling questions. They are questions that cut at the very heart of our American system. The apostle Paul talks about the lawfulness of government, but he does so with the assumption that government protects the innocent and punishes the guilty. God does not recognize the legitimacy of any other form of government.

"But government in America," writes Harold O.J. Brown, "is well on its way to standing the biblical requirement on its head, by protecting the guilty and punishing the innocent. . . . Faced with legal trends in

America that seem to turn fundamental biblical values upside down, we must in all seriousness ask the question of whether the basic policies of our government may not shortly become so perverted that it will be impossible to continue to credit its authority as coming from God."[2]

A frightening prospect. But as Jeremy Jackson points out in *No Other Foundation*, Christians in the Western world are "now in a considerable minority," and the law is changing accordingly, "to accommodate humanistic values." Drastic shifts in the law regarding abortion and captial punishment, for example, "illustrate the basic egocentrism of humanism which, by taking life lightly, will sentimentally preserve the murderer's life and callously commit a million fetuses to the hospital incinerators."[3]

Two questions must surely be asked.

First, how far has America come down this twisted path of human reasoning away from its foundations of biblical principles?

Second, who is responsible for where we are?

Our descent into judgment doesn't stop with immorality and the slaughter of innocents through abortion. We have come further and continue deeper. Just as in Hosea's time, "bloodshed follows bloodshed."

Now that we have rationalized and legalized the killing of the unborn, what is the next logical step?

The cry of the pro-abortionists is that every child should be a wanted child. And we have seen where that sweet-sounding but tragic reasoning leads— to the wholesale killing of "imperfect" fetuses in the womb. Someone might ask, "What about those children who have been born already and are imperfect?"

In his *Christian Manifesto,* Francis Schaeffer gives an example of the humanistic logic as it is expressed from an allegedly Christian viewpoint:

> An example of this coming down naturally on the side of the nonreligious humanists is the article by Charles Hartshorne in the January 21, 1981, issue of *The Christian Century,* pages 42-45. Its title is "Concerning Abortion, an attempt at a Rational View." He begins equating the fact that the human fetus is alive with the fact that mosquitoes and bacteria are also alive. That is, he begins by assuming that human life is not unique. He then continues by saying that *even after the baby is born* it is not fully human until its social relations develop (though he says the infant does have some primitive social relations an unborn fetus does not have). His conclusion is, "Nevertheless I have little sympathy with the idea that infanticide is just another form of murder. Persons who are already functionally persons in the full sense have more important rights even than infants."

Notice this key phrase, *"functionally persons."* This concept is an important step toward state-sanctioned killing of the elderly, the retarded, the crippled or emotionally ill—people who are "unable to function in a meaningful life." Again, the war of words.

Schaeffer continues:

> He then, logically, takes the next step: "Does this distinction apply to the killing of a hopelessly senile person or one in a permanent

coma? For me it does." No atheistic humanist could say it with greater clarity. It is significant at this point to note that many of the denominations controlled by liberal theology have come out, publicly and strongly, in favor of abortion.[4]

America's Surgeon General, Dr. C. Everett Koop, states:

By making abortion-on-demand the law of the land, the Supreme Court set the stage for infanticide and euthanasia: first the unborn were deprived of their right to life, then the recently born were classified as having no potential for meaningful life. . . .

Since infanticide is homicide and since all who practice it should be prosecuted, it is called "selection"—selection of some newborn babies to life and selection of others to death—usually by starvation (which to the surprise of many takes several weeks).

Infanticide is nothing more than euthanasia of the newly born. The next category of citizens in our country who might be classed as individuals having life not worthy to be lived is the elderly.

Euthanasia is the purposeful killing of a dependent human being, allegedly for his own good. Whether this death is accomplished by passive means such as withholding vital support or a direct action to terminate a life makes no difference; in either instance a life is terminated. The result of the euthanasia movement could well be an emphasis that shifts from the killing of

> an individual for the alleged benefit of that
> individual to the killing of an individual for
> the benefit of others.[5]

The situation has become extreme. Not only is man,
even Christian man, unsatisfied with the killing of
unborn life, but now he is pushing to legalize the murder
of those living, and all in the name of convenience. Again,
the "quality of life" ethic replaces the "sanctity of life"
ethic!

Often, the argument over sustaining life at all costs boils
down to just that—costs. Economics has become more
important than human life. It has come to "How much is
each life worth?" If an individual can live a productive
life, contributing to society and the state, then, maybe, he
can justify his existence. But, if he is unable to *produce*,
and if to invest care in him means no promise of return, his
life becomes, in society's eyes, valueless. Too often, life-
and-death situations are judged on the merits of their
convenience. If it is determined that caring for an
"imperfect" child or a "senile" adult is inconvenient for
the family, then maybe the answer is murder.

Such a time may not be as far away as we believe. "Right
to Die" movements are springing up everywhere. Is it so
hard to imagine a world where, when being admitted to a
hospital, we must sign consent forms stating that we agree
to be euthanized if the doctors determine it is our only
"cure"?

Joe Bayly has written a disturbing book entitled
Winterflight[6] that describes, through fiction, a future
where no "imperfect" children are allowed to be born, and
the aged are required to consent to death when they reach a
certain age. Bayly's book is fiction now, but it comes closer
and closer to being fact each day.

Our movement as a nation away from biblical precepts has not occurred overnight. Man has moved in to take God's place one step at a time. As each new advance in science occurs, man moves one more step toward his own supposed deity. Or rather, man becomes falsely self-confident, believing that he doesn't really need God anyway.

As Jackson put it:

> First and foremost, comes the denial of God's Word, subtly, then more openly. Then, each succeeding booster capitalizes upon this denial: the structures of life and thought which depend upon the Word of God are jettisoned. Finally, the witness of God's Word having become so attenuated, man is ready to embrace a system of values at total variance to his own created being. Given over to a reprobate mind, he accepts the worship of the Reprobate.[7]

Humanism teaches the absence of God in creation. Without God, there are no absolutes. Morality becomes a matter of situational ethics, and that even taken to an extreme. Man himself becomes the self-centered basis for morality and law. Law is made to equal morality. If it's legal, then it's right. This means that if prostitution is legalized it is morally right. And in one state and several other countries, it has been legalized. Since often the law reflects what society is already practicing, how long will it be before prostitution, marijuana and other drugs, and forms of pornography are legalized?

How is it possible that a country, supposedly founded on biblical principles, or at least on the belief that there were absolutes, gets to this point—especially when Christianity is such a visible and prevalent force as it is today?

One view is that, like the Israelites of Hoseas's time, we modern Christians have acquiesced to the pagans. The secular humanists made themselves sound intellectually well grounded to us; we forsook our biblical moorings. Secular humanism was made to sound convincing and logical, and biblical Christianity by contrast was painted as obsolete. Humanism became fashionable. The true gospel of Jesus became passé.

Another view is the concept a friend has termed the "wagons in a circle" mentality, or Christian "me-ism." Instead of actively engaging the world and the secular humanists with God's Word and law, we have withdrawn into our Christian ghettoes. In the face of the humanists' attack on the Gospel, we've drawn our wagons into a circle in a meager effort of self-defense. Or we've withdrawn into our Christian bookstores, Christian concerts, Christian theaters, Christian this and Christian that—while the world outside goes to hell. While there is nothing essentially wrong with any of these things, there is a problem in that they have all failed to confront the world where the world needs to be confronted.

The church has allowed the media to play havoc with the image of what Christians are. We are often appalled at the media's portrayal of what they believe a Christian to be. Indeed, they are showing us as we have appeared to them: squeamish, self-serving, and withdrawing—and, ultimately, unconvincing.

While the evangelicals of the church are making themselves more and more visible today, for decades only the liberals made themselves seen and heard. Sadly, the liberal church is nothing more than secular humanism dressed up in clerical robes. To the unwary, it may look and sound like Christianity, but underneath it is as empty as the rest of secularism. The liberal church has abdicated its position on true biblical morality to remain chic and acceptable to the world. They haven't withdrawn from moral battle; they simply haven't engaged in it.

As a result of this failure by the true church, secular society has followed through by disallowing the Christian voice. Christians have withdrawn from the scene as the secularists have gladly allowed them out.

Brown says it this way in *The Reconstruction of the Republic:*

> In America, Christians are custodians of the values of our civilization. If we exclude ourselves or allow ourselves to be excluded from participation in public policymaking whenever political and spiritual concerns overlap, then we are depriving our whole society of its richest source of ethical insight. . . . If the Christians, who have custody of the heritage, keep it under wraps and out of sight, then the debate on political and constitutional policies will be carried out largely in a vacuum. And this is precisely what is happening.
>
> The wasteland of values that exists in America today exists very largely as a result of the abdication of Christians. . . .
>
> Liberals, such as Arthur S. Flemming, chairman of the U.S. Civil Rights Commission and former president of the National Council of Churches, appear to be so dedicated to "pluralism" and the "separation of church and state" that instead of being advocates of the values they claim to hold, they actively work to exclude them from consideration when they are presented by others. . . . If the Christians will not advocate

their own value system, they certainly cannot expect others to do it for them. . . . The result, a combination of voluntary abdication of responsibility on the part of Christians and deliberate interference by some militant secularists, is what we may call the disfranchisement of Christians in America.[8]

In the relatively few instances where Christians have attempted to take a biblical stand against the forces of secular humanism, they have themselves been ensnared in semantic traps. Brown points out that pro-abortionists have often successfully lured biblical Christians into the argument that a fetus is not in fact "innocent human life in the Bible's sense." Large numbers of Christians, he observes, "have been reduced to silence by the slogan 'freedom of choice,' " a phrase that implies one person has no right to impose his morality on another—all to the exclusion of any consideration of the longing of God's heart.[9]

In spite of the "freedom of choice" argument, the secularists are militant in their advocacy of their interpretation of morality—which is really no morality at all. The secularist is exceedingly vocal in stating that individuals have the right to be homosexual; and not stopping there, they go on to advocate the acceptance of homosexuals as a political community.

They state that sexuality is a private and individual preference, whether homosexual or heterosexual, yet bring the matter graphically and loudly before the general public in a matter which can be considered nothing less than imposing.

A television program that advocates the acceptability of homosexuality is an imposition.

Music that speaks positively concerning the sensual pleasures of immorality in any form is an imposition when it is played over the public airwaves.

Magazines and books that advocate promiscuity, adultery, and all manner of immorality are an imposition.

And refusing to take a stand against such open advocacy of immorality in the name of "free speech" and other rights is sheer recklessness on the part of the church.

When virtue is absent, a moral vacuum is created. Immorality fills the gap. Man cannot live in a moral void. Without morality, he will turn to immorality.

Bernard Ramm, in his book *After Fundamentalism*, puts it this way:

> Those who want to make the good intrinsically good, and hence independent from God, turn ethics loose in the world like an orphan. Ethics is thus, expected to live on its own autonomous strength. Such a view of the separation of ethics and religion certainly pleases the philosophers, for they can give their lectures and write their books in happy isolation from troublesome religion. But such an orphan can hardly survive in any healthly way in the evil, wicked, depraved world, whose depravity is heavily documented by every daily edition of the newspaper. Fyodor Dostoyevsky wrote in *The Brothers Karamazov* that if there is no God nor immorality nor natural law, then it is entirely possible that all our vices could be converted into virtues. Even cannibalism could become a virtue. Such is the fate of morality if ethics is made an orphan. In the modern mood of the most extreme permissiveness in our society, Dostoyevsky's words are coming to pass.[10]

Who is responsible for this wholesale abandonment of biblical ethics and morality? Who is culpable for the crimes that have been committed against innocent lives slaughtered by the millions every year in the name of convenience?

The whole nation is responsible.

The church as a whole is responsible.

We are responsible.

Brown asks, quite rightly, if God refused to tolerate Nazism's extermination of six million Jews, why should we believe He will overlook our murdering of more than a million unborn babies per year?

We cannot escape the verdict that is coming against our society. We are guilty either of abandoning God's laws or tolerating the abandonment. In our situation, silence is just as condemning as active wrongdoing.

God made this clear long ago in Leviticus 20:1-5, when He told Moses to prohibit child sacrifices under penalty of death:

"If the people of the community close their eyes when that man gives one of his children to Molech and they fail to put him to death," the Lord added, "I will set my face against that man and his family and will cut off from their people both him and all who follow him in prostituting themselves to Molech."

We face judgment today, just as surely as Israel and Judah faced judgment then. And as the prophets detailed, that judgment came not only against the pagans, but also against the Israelites for following paganism, and against the priests for saying and doing nothing to turn the children of Israel back to God. The leaders, the kings, were condemned as well, as was the land itself.

Judgment was a collective, sweeping act.

"Don't point your finger at someone else, and try to pass the blame to him!" the Lord declares in Hosea 4:4-12 (Living Bible). "Look, priest, I am pointing my finger at *you*. . . . My people are destroyed because they don't know me, and it is all your fault, you priests, for you yourselves refuse to know me: therefore I refuse to recognize you as my priests. Since you have forgotten my laws, I will 'forget' to bless your children. . . .

"The priests rejoice in the sins of the people; they lap it up and lick their lips for more! And thus it is: 'Like priests, like people'—because the priests are wicked, the people are too. Therefore, I will punish both priests and people for all their wicked deeds. They will eat and still be hungry. Though they do a big business as prostitutes, they shall have no children, for they have deserted me and turned to other gods.

"Wine, women, and song have robbed my people of their brains. . . . Longing after idols has made them foolish."

Just because we are "the church," we have no special protection from God's judgment. Billy Graham states in *World Aflame*, "We cannot claim to be God's pets. We have no dispensation from judgment. If we continue in our present course, the moral law that says 'the wages of sin is death' (Rom. 6:23) will mean ultimate death to our society.[11]

But acknowledging our corporate guilt is not enough. In fact, doing so for some is just a way of shifting the blame to an "other." We point the finger at everyone, thus point it at no one, and nothing is resolved. The guilt still exists.

Says Brown,

> All people have a generalized sense of culpability, of *malaise*, but a knowledge of the

Law of God is required to bring this sense of culpability to a focus and to deal with it. This is precisely what our society does not want to hear; consequently, in increasing numbers we cannot deal with our sense of culpability, and resort to subterfuges such as confessing the whole nation guilty because of our affluence in an effort to escape guilt.[12]

Guilt displacement has become a fine art in modern times, but it has always existed. In Jeremiah 2:24, 25 (NIV), God confronts the illusion of innocence: "On your clothes men find the lifeblood of the innocent poor, though you did not catch them breaking in."

In other words, we don't even have a legitimate self-defense argument for our killing, such as the person surprised by a burglar in the night who kills to save his own life.

"Yet in spite of all this," the Lord continues, "you say, 'I am innocent; He is not angry with me.' But I will pass judgment on you, because you say, 'I have not sinned.' "

To point an accusing finger at "everybody"—at "America"—without accepting blame as individuals is hypocrisy in action. We cannot escape the truth that not only are we guilty as a corporate body (even if that body is the church), but we are guilty as individuals. Or, more clearly, we are responsible as individual Christians for the sins of our society.

As we have stood by and kept silent, and even participated in our society's materialistic idolatry and spiritual apostasy, we have come away with blood on our hands. That blood—innocent blood, shed by official sanction of a society that we as citizens control, blood shed by our complacency—cries to God for vengeance and vindication.

While we have spent our energies as a church on a hundred comparatively trivial issues, civilization has careened toward disaster. University of Iowa theologian George Forell has compared such non-essential movements to "rival deck stewards competing with each other about the arrangement of the deck chairs just before the Titanic hits the iceberg." [13]

"The crack in the moral dam is widening," Billy Graham has said, "but like the people of Noah's day before the flood, life goes on as usual with only a few concerned and scarcely anyone alarmed. However, apathy will not deter catastrophe. The people of Noah's day were not expecting judgment—but it came!"[14]

Will America learn from history?

Notes for Chapter Ten

[1] Thomas Nelson, 1983, p. 296.

[2] Harold O.J. Brown, *The Reconstruction of the Republic*, Mott Media, p. 119.

[3] Jeremy Jackson, *No Other Foundation*, Crossway Books, 1980, p. 162.

[4] Francis Schaeffer, *A Christian Manifesto*, Crossway Books, 1982, pp. 21-22.

[5] *Turning Point: Christian America at the Crossroads*, comp. Roger Elwood, Standard, 1980, pp. 46-47.

[6] Word Books, 1981.

[7] Jeremy Jackson, op. cit., p. 289.

[8] Brown, op. cit., pp. 127-128.

[9] Ibid., p. 137.

[10] Bernard Ramm, *After Fundamentalism*, Harper & Row, 1983, pp. 147-148.

[11] Billy Graham, *World Aflame*, Fleming H. Revell, 1965.

[12] Brown, op. cit., p. 20.

[13] "Reason, Relevance, and a Radical Gospel," *Against the World for the World*, ed. Berger and Newhaus.

[14] Graham, op. cit., p. 22.

AT THE ABYSS

If we are to be useful to Jesus Christ, it is essential that we perceive the idolatrous nature of our culture and react as His followers by opposing it. If we understand the Bible's message, we will be able to recognize that the *ancient forces of idolatry are as active today* as they were when the Bible was written.
—Joel Nederhood, *Freedom and Faith*[1]

America and Western society are on the brink of the abyss, headed for a descent into the depths of God's judgment. As Israel and Judah fell, so we are falling.

The catch phrases of the day tell our story. Every woman has the right to control her own body. A fetus is not a person. Every child should be a wanted child. Euthanasia of the hopelessly ill is "mercy killing." The anguish of aging and senility could be averted by voluntary death. Genetic engineering can yield a perfect humanity. The rights of individuals extend to the choice of sexual orientation and practice. Sexual license is a right. Homosexuality is an acceptable alternative lifestyle. Abortion on demand is a right.

And the secular litany continues, ad nauseum.

In *United Evangelical Action*, the official publication of the National Association of Evangelicals, David McKenna writes concerning the prophetic message for today:

> Jesus gives us the key for tuning our prophetic instruments and harmonizing our prophetic overture in the church today. . . .
>
> God himself steps into the heart of human existence in the presence of His Son and into the center of human culture with the principles of his kingdom. The pure prophetic note is always heard at the center of the individual and corporate soul in concrete and specific circumstances. . . .
>
> Through us, God wants to confront the secular counter-movement from the strategic center of society; with a public voice and against specific sins.
>
> . . . God's just and righteous character is the keynote to which society must be tuned, and the principles of justice in his kingdom are the notes on the chord which society must play.[2]

As was true in Hosea's day, the time for a call to repentance, a prophetic warning of impending judgment, is indeed at hand. The time and need for such a call could not be more apparent. The daily newspaper makes the case.

One newspaper describes the fight of a pro-abortionist United States Senator to defeat, once and for all, anti-abortion measures on the floor of the United States Senate.

The senator claims that the Right to Life movement "cannot sustain its zeal" and faces certain legislative defeat in "one last battle." He assesses the pro-life impact on the country as "minimal," and speaks highly of the *Roe v. Wade* decision by the Supreme Court which keeps abortions out of the "back rooms."

The article concludes with the notice that he "was honored Friday by the Religious Coalition for Abortion Rights in Washington for his role last year in 'leading the fight to defend religious and reproductive freedom.' "

In the March 2, 1983, issue of *USA Today,* four separate editorials discuss the "right to die" movement. One states that "Virginia became the 14th state to pass 'right to die' legislation. Fifteen other states are considering it. . . . It is a good idea, and more people should think about it."

In two of the editorials, Sidney Rosoff of the Euthanasia Society of America and Derek Humphry of the Hemlock Society briefly discuss their roles in "helping people to die," lauding assistance for people committing what is literally suicide (although they prefer to call it "dignified self-deliverance"), even describing such help as the "supreme act" of love for another.

Schlossberg has another disturbing angle:

> As the famous report to the Club of Rome explained it, the world's situation will worsen progressively with the rising population and will find relief only when the death rate increases.[3]
>
> Death, then, is the answer to our economic problems. The elderly will be called selfish if they insist on living, and it will be a humanitarian deed and moral duty to see that they do not continue to live and so deprive others of the quality of life to which they aspire. Some day, perhaps, Francis Crick's call for a new ethic that would insist on mandatory death for all

persons over eighty years of age will seem like a first hesitant step toward the brave new world that humanism is bringing into realization.[4]

Life magazine ran an article called "The Uterus as Operating Room" which speaks of the amazing advances medicine has made in diagnosing and treating various disorders in the fetus before birth. The article describes these innovations as being met with enthusiasm and hope by doctors and prospective parents alike, except in ethically questionable situations:

> Treating the unborn human beings opens a Pandora's box of ethical questions. At present, the largest branch of fetal medicine is prenatal diagnosis. By looking at a fetus's shape through ultrasound, examining its chromosomes through amniocentesis, or drawing a smidgen of its blood through fetoscopy, doctors can determine if it has any of more than 100 defects. Since parents often choose to terminate such a pregnancy, anti-abortionists have called these procedures "search-and-destroy missions." One of the most controversial cases was the "selective abortion" performed in 1981 at New York's Mount Sinai Hospital. The mother learned through early testing that she was carrying twins, one of whom had Down's syndrome. Should she keep both or abort both? Her doctors offered her a third, radical option: to destroy the damaged fetus by withdrawing its blood through a needle, while letting the other twin live. The prenatal operation succeeded, and the mother delivered one healthy baby and one *fetus papraceus*, a papery vestige of the organism that had been.[5]

As in Hosea's time, "bloodshed follows bloodshed." Society twists God's laws into nightmares. Even where God has offered the hope of saving life while in the womb, society has turned the hope into despair by offering death instead of life.

It is time for Christians to speak out as a body against the sins of society, the sins for which we also, as individuals, are responsible. Where society speaks about rights, we should speak back about responsibilities.

We have to move away from the "myth of neutrality." This is the myth society perpetuates that all views have equal merit. This has a ring of truth, but God's Word contradicts it. Christianity does not live in peaceful coexistence with godlessness. Accordingly, when a Christian speaks out, the response is often indignation and contempt. But still the call must go forth.

Franky's father, Francis Schaeffer, notes in his *Christian Manifesto* that for every three live births, one child is aborted. On the heels of this statistic, he issues a clarion call to the Bible-believing community:

> Christians must come to the children's defense, and Christians must come to the defense of human life as such.
>
> This defense should be carried out on at least four fronts:
>
> *First,* we should aggressively support a human life bill or a constitutional amendment protecting unborn children.
>
> *Second,* we must enter the courts seeking to overturn the Supreme Court's abortion decision.
>
> *Third,* legal and political action should be

taken against hospitals and abortion clinics that perform abortions.

Fourth, the State must be made to feel the presence of the Christian community.[6]

In summary, Christians must become actively engaged in speaking God's Word and the message of the Gospel into the ear of society. We must stand up against the abortionists. This type of action can take many forms:

• Call the church to lead the way in prayers of national repentance, just as Daniel, Nehemiah, and Isaiah did in Bible times.

• Call the church to accept her part of the guilt and arise to lead the way in changing the God-denying humanistic culture of modern America.

• Intercede in prayer for our nation. Pray for a change in laws, for the election of men who will pass laws banning abortion, for appointment of pro-life Supreme Court justices.

• Proclaim the Gospel of Christ to redeem as we preach on the issues of abortion, infanticide and euthanasia from our pulpits, in the light of God's judgment and biblical prophecy.

• Write letters to our Congressmen and other political representatives in the state and in our nation's capital.

• Write letters to the editors of our community newspapers, expressing our opinions concerning abortion as it is being practiced today in our areas.

• Join with other community and religious groups who are like-minded in preventing abortion on demand.

• Keep informed as to what is happening in our legislatures concerning the abortion issue.

• Speak about the issue of abortion to our friends

and neighbors, explaining with compassion how God's laws are being violated.

• Become involved in the political process, the judicial process, the legal process as participants—running for office, even at the local level, to begin a hands-on movement of Christians accomplishing change.

And there is more that each of us can do, individually and in organized groups.

One concerned citizen, Hilda Simon of New Paltz, New York, in a letter to *Human Events*, had several suggestions: One would be to change the word "abortion" to *"feticide."* Another would be to have Dr. Nathanson's sonogram of an abortion (referred to earlier) seen by high school students over the age of fourteen and by women contemplating an abortion, as well as having it released over television. She also urged consideration for legislation that would make aborting a fetus that can survive outside the womb an act of infanticide, and therefore subject to prosecution.

God's Word is clearly behind us. We have no reason to be hesitant or ashamed of our stance. Our mandate is to speak out against what we know to be an immoral situation.

We have more than the right to speak out, we have the responsibility. "Some Christians find it relatively easy to rid their minds of the Jewish slaughter by blaming it on Hitler's demonic hatred," says D. Bruce Lockerbie. "But this is a gross oversimplification. It ignores the shameful collaboration in genocide by representatives of the church in Germany who, by their silence if nothing else, acquiesced to the extermination plot."[7] Loving our neighbor is more than just "knowing" we love them. It involves expressing that love through our words and actions, and even warning them of the danger of our common situation.

Joe Bayly, writing in *Pastoral Renewal,* October, 1984, said: "When the Supreme Court declared abortion legal in 1973, there was no outcry from evangelical Protestants—including evangelical Protestant physicians. We had been accustomed to accept the government's moral judgments uncritically as God's will and, therefore, to be obeyed. Some protesting movements have arisen since then, but I doubt that more than a small minority of our pastors have preached against this evil."

Preachers are perhaps more guilty than any other group. We have been sidelined by every doctrinal fad that has come through, and instead of preaching the Word of God—so that people will truly come to *know God*—we preach the latest thing on the Christian market. We preach faith when faith is a popular topic, then shift to submission, then to church growth, then to success and prosperity. We preach prophecy, occupying ourselves with the *schedule* of the last days instead of proclaiming the crucial *message* of the last days.

May we preachers get alone in the Word and in prayer, and begin again to expound the Scriptures. Only from the Word of God will our people know God. The new "fad" ought to be biblical, expository—and impassioned—preaching.

"When I ordain a man as a priest," the Archbishop of Canterbury declared a few years ago, "I'm not looking for a good organizer, a financier, or an entertainer. I want a man who has seen the Lord and who has a gospel big enough for the world and its needs. . . . I need a minister who himself sweats to know the truth and to proclaim it."

Yes, we as the church must speak concerning the knowledge of God, of recovering an awareness of who God is, and then acting upon that awareness in every aspect of our lives.

We must not, however, fall into the judgmental stance ourselves. America doesn't need just another angry voice. *She needs the voice of grief.*

We must become a "crying church" for "crying sins"!

We are not, after all, the judges, but merely God's spokesmen. Acting and speaking as God's judges produces exactly the result we do not seek. "One of the ways we make void the word of God," Jeremy Jackson writes, "is by automatically identifying ourselves with God as judge, over against what or who is being judged."[8]

We must inspire man with God's dream. The time is now—but the hour is very, very late.

Listen to Schaeffer's ringing statement:

> I am convinced that one of the great weaknesses in evangelical preaching in the last few years is that we have lost sight of the biblical fact that man is wonderful. We have seen the unbiblical humanism which surrounds us, and, to resist this in our emphasis on man's lostness, we have tended to reduce man to a zero. Man is indeed lost, but that does not mean he is nothing. . . . To make a man a zero is neither the right way nor the best way to resist [humanism]. . . . The Christian position is that man is made in the image of God and, even though he is now a sinner, he can do those things that are tremendous—he can influence history for this life and the life to come, for himself and for others.[9]

We have received a charge to speak against sin and to call secular society away from its modern pursuit of paganism, but we are to do so with compassion and love. We must sound the trumpet of warning, yes. We must turn society back from the brink of destruction, yes, just as Hosea and other prophets did. But we are also to send a note of hope and joy. Every man, though fallen, still bears God's image. Let us inspire mankind again with God's dream. The gospel is the tremendous story of Christ's redeeming us back to God's dream.

Let's lead in the celebration of life!

And before we can preach to society a message of repentance, we ourselves must first repent. We must seek God's face and His forgiveness for our past silence and complacency. We have only ourselves to blame for allowing society to come so far. Had the call been sounded firmly and clearly in past decades, America's condition would not be so tragic today. We must repent, and then revival will come to our nation.

On the other hand, "To preach repentance to get revival would be a barren procedure," Jackson correctly points out in *No Other Foundation*. "The real preaching of repentance issues from repentance, just as the real preaching of joy and victory only carries conviction when it results from joy and victory."[10]

May our churches recover the awareness of God's glory in their meetings. It makes little sense for preachers and churches to rail at the world about their sins, unless the glory of God is in their midst—for in that glory is the power of conviction, and therein lies the hope for change.

The effects of our culture's disobedience are all around us. We have all been touched by the sins of our society. If we ourselves have not been involved in the immorality of the world, we know friends and relatives who have been. We know others caught in the web of sin. And we know of those who have aborted their children.

Having ourselves received God's forgiveness, and experiencing His compassion, we ought to turn to offer that same compassion to others. "Freely you have received, freely give."

We must call sin "sin." But we must also love. Most important, there is hope!

Raising our voices against abortion, and any of the other evidences of the twin sins, will not be easy. But we cannot allow ourselves to be easily silenced. We must strike the tents of silence and march into the battle with the authority of God's Word as our weapon.

To sit in silence means entering obscurity. If we do not speak out against the sin around us, against the shedding of innocent blood, we will become obscure as we suffer the judgment of God along with our idolatrous culture. We will become the victims of our own passiveness, our own apostasy, and thus co-conspirators with the idolatry and sin of our society.

Whittier wrote:

> Is the old Pilgrim spirit quench'd within us?
> Stoops the proud manhood of our souls so low,
> That Mammon's lure or Party's wile can win
>   us to silence now?
> Now, when our land to ruin's brink is verging.
> In God's name let us speak while there is time:
> Now, when the padlocks for our lips are forging,
> *Silence is a crime.*

Jeremy Jackson notes that "the cultivation of sin is always easier than its eradication. . . . The cost of dealing with sin is very great. The living proof is our Lord and Saviour who suffered a death unimaginable in its dimensions in order to redeem creation from the effects of our disobedience. The root of all fruitful mission and all effective social work is in a serious emulation of

Christ—becoming like him in his death, sharing in his sufferings, as Paul put it."[11]

We must also be careful not to give "popular" or watered-down answers to our nation's woes. Many are offering such. The popular book *When Bad Things Happen to Good People,* written by a rabbi, talks of God as if He were feeble, limited in how He can move among His people. Charles Colson, commenting on the book, says it has achieved such popularity because there is such a lack of knowledge in our society concerning God and His Word. Colson cites Gallup reports from 1963 which indicated that sixty-three percent of all Americans believed the Bible to be God's Word, while today the figure is only thirty-seven percent.

Colson asks the pointed question, "If we don't proclaim the Truth, who will?" Schlossberg reminds us that "One major function fo the church is to unmask the idols and expose them for what they are."

God will not tolerate our nation's sin, and neither will He tolerate our silence towards it. Our silence is nothing more than a visible sign of our lack of compassion for our neighbor. We must be moved to speak the truth and to speak it now.

As Schaeffer and Koop write in *Whatever Happened to the Human Race?*: "If we ache and have compassion for humanity today in our own country and across the world, we must do all we can to help people see the truth of Christianity and accept Christ as Savior. And we must stand against the loss of humanness in all its forms. . . . In the end we must realize that the tide of humanism, with its loss of humanness, is not merely a cultural ill, but a spiritual ill that Christ alone can cure."[12]

Should we face judgment? Augustine, one of the church fathers, observed that for God to allow crimes and vices to go unpunished is a more terrible judgment than for Him to curb them by affliction.

The prospect of God's final judgment is frightening. Gary Bergel, director of Intercessors for America, writes a compelling sentence upon mankind:

> We have cursed ourselves and our national life. As a result, we will continue to find upheaval around every corner. We will move from crisis to crisis rather than from glory to glory (Gen. 9:5-7, Levi. 18:21-29).
>
> A cry is now mounting for "Peace!" We are afraid. We want to preserve ourselves and our children from nuclear holocaust. . . .
>
> If God, who is sovereign, should allow the devastation of a nuclear exchange, I am personally convinced that He would be justified in the bringing of this judgment on the basis of abortion alone.
>
> What audacity we have—to ask Him to keep us and our "planned" families alive while condoning the grossest execution of one fourth of our children—His inheritance—over the past ten years! We cry for peace while we unrelentingly war against and exterminate the unborn of our species! We have become a deceived and foolish people.[13]

America has reached the brink of the abyss. Only a genuine spiritual and moral renewal can prevent God's judgment from wasting the land.

Notes for Chapter Eleven

[1] Ed. Lynn Buzzard, Crossway Books, 1982.

[2] David McKenna in *United Evangelical Action*, National Association of Evangelicals, Winter 1982.

[3] See Eliot Slater, "Health Service or Sickness Service," *British Medical Journal*, 1971, No. 4, p. 735.

[4] Herbert Schlossberg, *Idols for Destruction*, Thomas Nelson, 1983, pp. 233-234.

[5] Anne Fadiman, "The Uterus as Operating Room," *Life*.

[6] Francis Schaeffer, *A Christian Manifesto*, Crossway Books, 1982, pp. 118-120.

[7] D. Bruce Lockerbie, "Laughter Without Joy: The Burlesque of Our Secular Age," *Christianity Today*, October 7, 1977, p. 15.

[8] Jeremy Jackson, *No Other Foundation*, Crossway Books, 1980.

[9] Francis Schaeffer, *Death in the City*, Inter-Varsity Press, 1969, pp. 80-81.

[10] Jackson, op. cit., p. 215.

[11] Ibid., p. 258.

[12] Francis Schaeffer and C. Everett Koop, *Whatever Happened to the Human Race?* Fleming H. Revell, 1979, p. 198.

[13] Gary Bergel, "Abortion: A Biblical Issue That Must Be Resolved," *A.L.L. About Issues*, 1983, p. 16.

GOD OF THE "ONCE MORE"

> The prophet is a man of deep pathos in
> the classic sense of the word, which means
> "suffering." He suffers with his people, for his
> people, and because of his people. *Above all, he
> suffers with God and for God*, because sin and
> unrighteousness alienate the people from their
> holy God.
>
> —Dr. Victor Buksbazen

If there is a bottom line to the prophetic message of the
Scriptures for our age, it is not a message of anger, or of
despair, or of disaster—but of hope.

In spite of all the stormy accusations and warnings
throughout the prophetic books of the Bible, there is
always a redeeming at the end. God always holds out that
final glimmer of hope.

Nowhere is this truth more poignantly expressed than
in the touching, tragic story of Gomer and Hosea. It is a
love story, a picture of God's love for Israel, and thereby a
picture of God's love for us today.

Some scholars regard Hosea and Gomer's story as the
second-greatest story in the Bible, next only to the account

of the passion of our Lord in His life and work of Redemption given in the gospels. Hosea and Gomer's story is a powerful, gripping drama centered around the most intimate of human relationships. It is a pageant that uses as illustrations both Hosea and Gomer's children, and their own broken and restored marriage to portray the dealings of God with the sinning nation of Israel.

As such, therefore, this classic story becomes very important for us today to examine closely. There are two especially significant reasons for this. One is that we also live in a day when "bloodshed follows bloodshed," as Hosea did. We also live in "last days."

With this in mind, we might well ask: What might God say to us today? This is an excellent question. The answer to that can be discovered by answering a second question: *What has He already said?*

And one significant answer to that is the dynamic message in the Book of Hosea. This book was God's powerful, personal—and final—response to Israel's idolatrous, insensitive, immoral, murderous culture in those critical, decisive years just before the nation, under the judgment of God, fell to the Assyrians. This is important as the message can significantly instruct us today; so let us listen to it intently.

The other reason—and a vital one for us today—is what the story of Hosea *reveals about the character of God*. With our culture laden with sins such as abortion, immorality, idolatry, insensitivity, homosexuality, and division, it is paramount for us today to hear, clearly and earnestly, deep aspects of the character of God, our heavenly Father. These the message of Hosea provides in a very poignant way.

Any one of us might view Israel's culminating sins and react by thundering out proclamations of judgment.

But not God! No, Hosea reveals our Father's great heart of love, His compassion and mercy, His gracious call for repentance from His people so as to avert judgment.

Yes, the proclamations of judgment are in Hosea, but they are there in the context of God's loving grief:

> When Israel was a child I loved him . . . But the more I called Israel, the further they went from me. . . . My people are determined to turn from me. . . .
>
> How can I give you up, Ephraim? How can I hand you over, Israel? How can I treat you like Admah? How can I make you like Zeboiim? My heart is changed within me; all my compassion is aroused (Hos. 11:1, 2, 3, 8 NIV).

God doesn't want them to be judged; He wants them restored to blessing.

We can learn much from the story of Hosea, because this story shows us *who* God is! His heart's desire is to heal and redeem His people "once more."

Hosea, the son of Beeri, lived during the reign of Uzziah, Jotham, Ahaz, and Hezekiah, who were kings over Judah. During the same time, Jeroboam was king of Israel.

Halfway through the eighth century B.C., the nation began to crumble, and Jeroboam's reign was coming to a conclusion. Assyria, a country to the northeast, was rising in power. Little did the people of Israel realize that within a generation after the preaching of Hosea, Assyria would invade their country, and Israel would fall!

At the time Hosea was called to preach, the country had no sense of impending doom. Rather, the culture seemed to flourish and all seemed well. Peace was on the land.

The children of Israel were a covenant people. They were living under the divine covenant of God. The relationship that this entailed is described clearly in Deuteronomy 7:6-11:

> For you are a holy people to the Lord your God; the Lord your God has chosen you to be a people for Himself, a special treasure above all the peoples on the face of the earth.
>
> The Lord did not set His love on you nor choose you because you were more in number than any other people, for you were the least of all peoples; but because the Lord loves you, and because He would keep the oath which brought you out with a mighty hand, and redeemed you from the house of bondage, from the hand of Pharaoh king of Egypt.
>
> Therefore know that the Lord your God, He is God, the faithful God who keeps covenant and mercy for a thousand generations with those who love Him and keep His commandments; and He repays those who hate Him to their face, to destroy them. He will not be slack with him who hates Him; He will repay him to his face.
>
> Therefore you shall keep the commandment, the statutes, and the judgments which I command you today, to observe them.

What is the covenant of love? It is like a marriage covenant. God was saying to the children of Israel that they were spiritually married. They were the bride and God is the bridegroom. This same type of symbolism is used throughout the New Testament to describe the relationship between Christ and His Church.

The nation of Israel was very special. They were to be a people to receive God's mercy and His love. He would lavish on them His care, His blessings. The Israelites were God's chosen people, intended to be a blessing *to the entire world!* God's blessings upon them, and His care for them, were for that end.

The same is true of the church today. Christians, as a body, are God's chosen people.

"But you are a chosen generation," 1 Peter 2:9 (NKJV) declares, "a royal priesthood, a holy nation, His own special people, that you may proclaim the praises of Him who called you out of darkness into his marvelous light."

Israel's relationship with God was literally a "marriage made in heaven." One would expect Israel to be proud of such an intimate relationship with God. Surely they would protect their covenant and observe carefully each of God's laws, to preserve their well-being. But such was not the case.

It often happens when God's people experience His blessings and all is going well: we tend to forget who is behind the blessings. We lose our "knowledge of God." Just as Hosea warns, "there is no . . . knowledge of God in the land."

The Israelites, having their needs amply met, turned away from God and toward their newly discovered idols. God became unnecessary. Who needed God, when man could do so well without Him?

The children of Israel didn't completely dispense with God. To some degree they retained the forms of their worship. But they also began to adopt the pagan forms of worship. They attempted to adapt their worship of God to fit the pagan culture around them in order to be socially acceptable.

It was here that they began "falsely worshiping the true God, and truly worshiping the false gods." John Updike, describes modern man's view of God. One of his characters

159

refers to God's presence as the same as "a pebble under the car seat." Modern man is vaguely aware of God's existence, but denies Him just the same by ignoring Him. It is ignorance of God—a lack of "the knowledge of God." It is not just a passive ignorance, but rather active rebellion against the light of revelation, suppression of the truth, as Romans 1 describes it.

The parallels between Bible times and modern times are disturbing. The liberal church has fallen into an apostate form of worship, attempting to merge God-less aspects of society with God's Word. When the Israelites became caught up in the paganism of their day, they not only sacrificed their children, but they sacrificed the sanctity of their covenant relationship with God. As Hosea graphically put it, they became spiritual whores and harlots, prostituting themselves to idols, committing spiritual adultery. They were a faithless bride to their bridegroom, God.

Hosea's description goes on to become even more revealing: "Your faithfulness," he writes, "is like a morning cloud, and like the early dew it goes away" (Hos. 6:4 NIV). They tried to keep up appearances before God, but it was a transparent foolishness that evaporated quickly under the Lord's close scrutiny.

And the initial involvement with pagan worship did not stop there. As the scriptural record shows, Israel moved deeper and deeper into darkness, allowing themselves to be seduced by the glamor of the pagan ritual. This worship then bore other fruit—as sin in any form does—including injustice, oppression of the poor, stealing, dishonesty and sexual immorality.

And then the bloodshed.

Friend killed friend, kings killed kings, robbers murdered their victims, and on and on. This moral drift culminated in the ultimate debasement of human life, the sacrifice of children to idols. The children of Israel, the covenant people, were now guilty of the most terrible and heinous crimes and sacrilege.

Sin now had an awful momentum of its own. The people began pushing beyond even reasonable civilized limits. "By swearing and lying, killing and stealing and committing adultery," Hosea 4:2 (NKJV) says, *"they break all restraint."*

The prophets preached their message of repentance, of judgment, and of hope, urging God's covenant people to turn away from their sins and return to the God who so loved them. Judgment is not God's motive; love is His motive. Judgment is the necessary outgrowth of continued rebellion. God's heart longed for a restored covenant with His people.

In the act of officially sanctioned child sacrifice, Israel committed the worst of immoralities. And yet God wanted to give them one more chance. He wanted to reach them once more.

God is a God of the "once more."

He wanted to reach their hearts, to touch the sinning people and claim them back to himself. He longed for His wayward bride.

The same is true today. God is always ready and eager to forgive and recover lost souls and lost nations. While sin's wages are death, God's Word offers the hope of forgiveness for the repentant.

"If we confess our sins," the Bible reminds us, "He is faithful and just to forgive us our sins and to cleanse us from all unrighteousness" (1 John 1:9 NKJV).

In the scriptural account, God needed a plan to recall Israel from their sin. He wanted to get their attention and remind them of their covenant relationship with Him.

The plan had to confront the people strongly, to jolt them and expose their sin. It had to make God's great love for them obvious and dramatically visible. It had to graphically portray His repugnance to their sin, their crucial role as His bride, the deep hurt that they had inflicted on God, and how desperate their plight truly was.

This was where Hosea came on the scene.

Hosea, the final prophet to Israel before their downfall, was God's tool for attempting to redeem Israel "once more" before He let His judgment fall.

As for the graphic "visual aid" designed to jolt Israel awake, God directed Hosea toward an unusual relationship, even while He was calling the man into the ministry: "Go take yourself a wife of harlotry," God said to Hosea, "and children of harlotry, for the land has committed great harlotry by departing from the Lord" (Hos. 1:2 NKJV).

Not only was Hosea called to preach God's warning to the fallen culture of Israel, but he was called to live out a metaphor of God's love, of judgment and restoration. Through his example, there would be no uncertainty as to what God had to say to His people.

Hosea followed God's instructions: "He went and took Gomer the daughter of Diblaim, and she conceived and bore him a son" (Hos. 1:4 NKJV). Hosea's marriage to Gomer was God's way of calling sin by its correct name. One of the most difficult tasks of the church is getting people to call sin "sin."

Some scholars believe that when Hosea first married Gomer, she was not already a promiscuous person. But, as we all have the potential for sin, she had the potential for her adultery. And commit adultery she did. Apparently, she became involved in the temple prostitution and Baal worship along with others in her culture. Just as Israel had committed double sins of idolatry and immorality, so did Gomer. She sinned against God and against Hosea. Gomer was a striking parallel for Israel's sin.

But Hosea's wife was not the only family member involved in this drama. The children were also included. First came Jezreel, whose name God had chosen deliberately:

Call his name Jezreel,
For in a little while
I will avenge the bloodshed of Jezreel on the house of Jehu,
And bring an end to the kingdom of the house of Israel.
It shall come to pass in that day
That I will break the bow of Israel in the Valley Jezreel
(Hos. 1:4, 5 NKJV).

Jezreel is a fascinating word which can mean two things: "God scatters" or "God sows." Both meanings are typified by the motion of a farmer's hand as he broadcasts seed. Ironically, this hand motion can be taken negatively, meaning "get away," or positively, related to planting. God's choice of the name Jezreel is a divine play on words, and both meanings come into play in the story of Hosea.

Jezreel is not only the name of Hosea's firstborn. It is also the name of a place. It was in Jezreel, years before, where the innocent owner of a vineyard, Naboth, was slain by the wicked King Ahab and Queen Jezebel. Naboth's innocent blood cried out to God to be avenged, and a man named Jehu was sent to do the job. But in the process of completing his mission, Jehu also shed innocent blood. When God says, "I will avenge the bloodshed of Jezreel on the house of Jehu," He is referring specifically to this actual historical event.

The name Jezreel, then, brings to mind two opposite images: one of vengeance for the shedding of innocent blood ("God scatters"), another of new life ("God sows"). Wrapped up in the name of Hosea's firstborn are *both* terror and hope.

Then there was Hosea's second-born, a daughter. Once again, God had picked out a name:

Call her name Lo-Ruhamah,
For I will no longer have mercy on the house of Israel,
But I will utterly take them away.
Yet I will have mercy on the house of Judah,
Will save them by the Lord their God,
And will not save them by bow,
Nor by sword or battle,
By horses or horsemen (Hos. 1:6, 7 NKJV).

Lo-Ruhamah means "no mercy." Here was God's indictment, stating that His mercy was going to be withdrawn in the face of Israel's continuing sins. What an awful consequence for the Israelites to face—no mercy! Not the mercilessness of an unfeeling God, but the direct result of man's choice to turn away from Him.

Finally, a third child was born to Hosea and Gomer:

Call his name Lo-Ammi,
For you are not my people,
and I will not be your God (Hos. 1:9 NKJV).

The third child's name bears the awful meaning of "not my people." To be called "my people" by the Lord God is an unequalled honor. For generations, Israel had been God's chosen people. Now, in one stroke, all that was undone in the naming of this child.

It was a prediction of judgment.

"Judgment is inseparable from idolatry," Schlossberg writes. "Human actions have moral consequences. There is a principle of moral accountability in the universe."[1]

But God's statement of condemnation did not stop with Lo-Ammi—"not my people." As if He was completely embarrassed by the nation's wickedness, God said He would no longer be their God. He would give them up to false gods. Let *them* take care of the people!

It is only when He has withdrawn from us that we fully feel the need of His presence, and our need of serving the One True God.

"Instead of balls of fire hurled down from above or visitations of plagues and boils, perhaps God is simply allowing us to wallow helplessly in the mire of our sin," writes Charles Colson. "Augustine's statement, 'The punishment of sin is sin,' captures the essence of this kind of judgment. The apostle Paul explained to the Romans how the sinful are cast out and punished: not by exterior censure, but by a rotting from within."[2]

Now Hosea's drama began in earnest; all the players were in place. The children were born and a true family was established.

But Gomer became seduced by the cultic worship. She attended the worship of idols, possibly even the sacrifices of children, and gave herself to the temple priests in pagan prostitution.

Soon, Gomer's spiritual and moral harlotry took its toll on the family. Hosea's heart was breaking. Still, he spoke out according to God's direction:

> Bring charges against your mother,
> bring charges;
> For she is not my wife,
> nor am I her husband!
> Let her put away her harlotries
> from her sight,
> And her adulteries from between her breasts;

Lest I strip her naked
And expose her, as in the day she was born,
And make her like a wilderness,
And set her like a dry land,
And slay her with thirst (Hos. 2:2, 3 NKJV).

This is an echo of the record of Hosea's children. Hosea was speaking not only of his personal situation, but also as the prophet of God speaking to the wayward covenant people. Hosea, like God, had lost his bride. He, like God, had been merciful, but now he threatened to withdraw that mercy. And Hosea, like God, finally declared that he was no longer a husband to the bride. Hosea was declaring "Lo-Ammi." So was God.

The larger tragedy of Hosea's life story is that Israel did not heed God's dramatic warning. Neither did Gomer. Both fell even deeper into sin. Gomer, going beyond the immorality of the temple, took her adultery to the streets, "chasing after her lovers" (Hos. 2:4, 5). She was no longer content for them to find her, but her passion was such that she now had to seek them out. She decked herself out in her best jewelry and clothes and took to the streets.

Israel did the same as a nation. The people continued their spiritual and moral whoring, while the immorality of the pagan temples overflowed into the community. In chapter four, Hosea described the many types of violence and sin that crop up as a result.

Hosea was slow to respond, hoping against hope that things were not really as corrupt as he suspected. But he noticed that Gomer was gone much of the time. Money was missing from the house. She came in late. Soon Hosea realized how totally unfaithful Gomer had been.

Imagine the gossip this leading preacher of the day must have endured! Every time folks talked about Gomer or

Hosea, their raised their eyebrows or snickered in disgust. She was a scandal.

Eventually, Gomer left the home completely, forsaking her husband, deserting her children, to spend more time whoring. Hosea was crushed. His soul burst with pain. He loved her still—just as God always loves His people.

The situation turned sour for Gomer, however, as well, just as it would for Israel. For God declares:

> Therefore, behold,
> I will hedge up your way with thorns,
> And wall her in,
> So that she cannot find her paths,
> She will chase her lovers,
> But not overtake them;
> Yes, she will seek them, but not find them
> (Hos. 2:6, 7 NKJV).

Suddenly, in the midst of her whoring, in the midst of openly defying her marriage vows, Gomer's situation took a nasty turn. She ran short of money. She couldn't pay the rent on her room. She hadn't enough food to eat. She couldn't afford the perfumes and make-up and new clothes that her profession required. She had spent everything in her sinning and her chasing after sin.

She became tired and worn. Her work exhausted her, and she could only respond to her poverty by working more, exhausting herself further. She spent time with more and more men, hoping they would give her money and gifts enough to get by. But they were just using her, and she hardly had the strength to collect her fees by force.

Finally, broken, destitute, her lewdness exposed, Gomer somehow fell into slavery.

And she was placed on the auction block.

Hers was the fate that awaited Israel, if they continued to ignore God's message. The pattern is clear: first mercy is withdrawn; then their title as God's people is taken away; next, God turns away from them in shame; and finally, they are to become slaves to the Assyrians, totally disgraced.

Here was a once proud nation, impervious to foreign aggression, having defeated every enemy with bold authority. Now they were put up on the auction block as slaves.

They ignored God's warnings as prophesied so clearly through Hosea. They continued their sinning, chasing ever more passionately after their false gods and immoral practices. To the end, they continued sacrificing their children to Molech.

Gomer is a picture of Old Testament Israel. Old Testament Israel is a picture of the modern United States.

Our nation stands in the same position today: we have one foot on the auction block. We are turning further and further from the commands of God. Society openly condones and promotes promiscuous and adulterous sex, homosexuality, euthanasia, abortion, infanticide, and pornography. Insensitivity, violence, and injustice are commonplace. The poor are a growing number. Just as Hosea charged, "The land has committed great harlotry . . . by departing from the Lord" (Hos. 1:2).

Will America and Western society listen to the prophetic warning? Will the church turn from consorting with the world to confronting the world? Will we call sin "sin"?

Will we, as responsible Christians, raise our voices against the awful sin of the death cries of millions of innocent babies aborted annually? Or will we claim false innocence, point our fingers at the collective nation, and ignore the country's slide toward judgment?

Will we too find ourselves in Israel's predicament because we have committed the ultimate crime?

Will America and Western society discover itself being sold at auction, a nation of slaves, under the rule of tyrants?

Or will the lesson of pitiful Gomer sink in?

Just like Israel, we are confronted with the spectre of God calling us "not my people," telling us to expect "no mercy," and leaving us to face the terror of His wrath—by the absence of His supernatural protection.

But there is more to the story of Hosea and Gomer.

Because He loves His people, God will never forsake His people. His mercy is everlasting and longsuffering. In Hosea 2:14 God said, "Therefore, I will allure her, will bring her into the wilderness, and will comfort her." The promise of God's love was still there, even to the point where He actively sought to redeem His people. It's not just a matter of us finding God. God is already reaching out to us. He is right beside us, pursuing us, waiting for us to turn back.

Hosea 3 tells of God's great mercy:

> The Lord said to me, "Go, show your love to your wife again, though she is loved by another and is an adulteress. Love her as the Lord loves the Israelites, though they turn to other gods. . . ."
>
> So I bought her for fifteen shekels of silver and about a homer and a lethek of barley. Then I told her, "You are to live with me many days; you must not be a prostitute or be intimate with any man, and I will live with you."
>
> For the Israelites will live many days without king or prince, without sacrifice or sacred

stones, without ephod or idol. Afterward the Israelites will return and seek the Lord their God and David their king. They will come trembling to the Lord and to his blessings in the last days.

God's love extended even to the still-sinning nation. Even though Israel failed to heed His warnings and fell to the Assyrians, yet God promised to restore them to himself. Even though they assured their own judgment by their own choice, God offered hope, restoration and redemption.

As a living example, Hosea did as God directed. He went out and searched for Gomer. He did not wait for her to return, but sought her out while she was yet in sin. He discovered her while she was enduring her judgment.

And, out of his undying love for his wife, Hosea bought her out of slavery and restored her to himself. In spite of her sin, she was still the love of his life.

It is one of the greatest themes of the Bible, and one of the highest virtues: *it is forgiveness.*

Hosea's dream was a marriage restored to its original fullness. God's dream is a people restored to their original covenant.

God's love for us flows from His dream for us. We break His heart, but we never shatter His dream.

When we come to Him, *He "once more" heals us.*

Notes for Chapter Twelve

[1] Herbert Schlossberg, *Idols for Destruction*, Thomas Nelson, 1983, p. 293.

[2] Charles Colson, "The Most Fearsome Judgment," *Christianity Today*, August 8, 1982, p. 21.

A CRYING PEOPLE

As He approached Jerusalem and saw the
city, He wept over it. . . . "Oh Jerusalem,
Jerusalem, you who kill the prophets . . . how
often I have longed to gather your children
together . . . but you were not willing."
— Luke 19:41; Matt. 23:37

As we speak to our world's sins we must speak as Hosea
and the prophets spoke—forcefully, candidly, yet with a
broken heart, full of compassion and love. And we must
not only speak to our world, but also to hurting
individuals.

Abortion is not an opportunity for finger-pointing and
condemnation. It is a time for taking the world by the
hand and leading the way back to God.

It is especially a time to reach out to women who have
been scarred by abortion and are carrying the pain of guilt.
Certainly, many women profess little guilt over their
abortion; however, millions express much guilt, and they
need the ministry of Christ's love and forgiveness. This is
also a time to help women who are struggling with a crisis
pregnancy, providing them an alternative to abortion as
well as loving counsel and emotional support.

As the church, we must reach out both to our world and to individuals with the same love Hosea expressed for Gomer, the same love that God expressed for Israel. It was a compassionate love, a love full of authority. It was a love that paved the way for repentance, not rebellion. It was love that knew the *"grief of God"*—grief being *"love's response to sin"* !

With such an attitude we become *"a crying people"* for *"crying sins"* !

A crying people are gripped with three realities:

One, the grievous sin of their culture.

Two, the powerful mercy of God who is ready to forgive society's sins when they repent.

And, three, the sobering reality of judgment if sin is not repented of.

In their concern over our world's wholesale shedding of innocent blood, crying people deeply realize that in the issue of abortion we today are playing with a loaded gun.

Such was the sober conviction of an early American minister, Jonas Clark, who, in a sermon in 1776 said: "Injustice, oppression, and violence—*much less the shedding of innocent blood*—shall not pass unnoticed by the just Governor of the world. Sooner or later, a just recompense will be made upon such workers of iniquity."[1]

The scene of impending judgment shown in vision to the prophet Ezekiel shook him and he cried to God: "Are you going to destroy the entire remnant of Israel in this outpouring of your wrath on Jerusalem?" And God answered: "The sin of the house of Israel and Judah is exceedingly great; the land is full of bloodshed and the city is full of injustice" (Ezek. 9:8, 9 NIV).

But the bright note is that first Ezekiel was shown those

who were praying—the crying people: "Go throughout the city of Jerusalem and put a mark on the foreheads of those who grieve and lament over the detestable things that are done in it" (Ezek. 9:4 NIV).

Ezekiel addressed the public of his day with words intended to be a trumpet call, an alarm to awaken his generation to repentance:

> This is what the Sovereign Lord says . . . The end! The end has come upon the four corners of the land. The end is now upon you and I will unleash my anger against you. . . . Prepare chains, because the land is full of bloodshed, and the city is full of violence (7:1-3, 23 NIV).

> Must they also fill the land with violence and continually provoke Me to anger? (8:17 NIV).

> You have killed many people in this city and filled its streets with the dead (11:6).

> And you took your sons and daughters whom you bore to me and sacrificed them as food to the idols. Was your prostitution not enough? You slaughtered my children and sacrificed them to the idols. . . . Because you poured out your wealth, and exposed your nakedness in your promiscuity with your lovers, and because of all your detestable idols, and because you gave them your children's blood . . . I will sentence you to the punishment of women who commit adultery and who shed blood. I will bring upon you the blood vengeance of my wrath and jealous anger (16:20-22, 35-38 NIV).

> When you offer your gifts—the sacrifice of your sons in the fire—you continue to defile yourselves with all your idols to this day (20:31 NIV).

Woe to the city of bloodshed . . . For the blood she shed is in her midst . . . Woe to the city of bloodshed! (24:6, 7, 9 NIV).

I will give you over to bloodshed and it will pursue you. Since you did not hate bloodshed, bloodshed will pursue you (35:6 NIV).

Then the summary of the reason for the judgment: "So I poured out my wrath on them because they had shed blood in the land and because they had defiled it with their idols" (36:18 NIV).

Ezekiel was also shown God looking for a crying people: "I looked for a man among them who would build up the wall and stand before me in the gap on behalf of the land so I would not have to destroy it, but I found none" (22:30 NIV).

The significance of this statement to us is diminished unless we realize that over and again, in the verses leading up to it in chapter twenty-two, Ezekiel indicted Jerusalem for her bloodshed:

The Word of the Lord came to me: "Son of man, will you judge her? Will you judge this city of bloodshed? Then confront her with her detestable practices and say,

"This is what the Sovereign Lord says: 'O city that brings on herself doom by shedding blood in her midst and defiles herself by making idols, you have become guilty because of the blood you have shed and have become defiled by the idols you have made. You have brought your days to a close, and the end of your years has come. . . .

" 'See how each of the princes of Israel who are in you uses his power to shed blood. . . . In you are slanderous men bent on shedding blood. . . . In you men accept bribes to shed blood. . . . I will surely strike my hands together . . . at the blood you have shed in your midst . . . . They shed blood and kill people to make unjust gain.' "

Since there were no crying people, judgment came: "So I will pour out my wrath on them and consume them with my fiery anger, bringing down on their own heads all they have done!" (Ezek. 22:31 NIV).

Will we become a crying people for crying sins? If we do, we will begin to storm the gates of Hell in prayer and intercession. We will recognize that the first battle is spiritual. This is because sins such as abortion—or any evidence of the twin sins, or other sins—are expressions of the larger satanic entrenchment of our God-denying culture: "For our struggle is not against flesh and blood, but against the rulers, against the authorities, against the powers of this dark world and against the spiritual forces of evil in the heavenly realm" (Eph. 6:12 NIV).

But an issue is needed to jolt God-fearing people to action. Could abortion be that issue, the issue which finally stirs the church into forceful spiritual warfare?

Could abortion be the issue which jolts the church at last to speak up in the public arena, insisting that our laws reflect the sanctity-of-life ethic instead of sanctioning the shedding of innocent blood?

Could abortion be the issue that effectively humbles God-fearing people to lead the way in repentance for our culture's sins? May pastors, priests and rabbis take the initiative!

Could abortion be the issue that shakes us to earnestly minister God's love to those who have been wounded by abortion?

Could abortion—ironically in this case—be the issue that stirs us to joyfully celebrate life—life given to us by God—and to look at one another with new eyes that see each person "as an unrepeatable miracle?"

The issue that stirred us could have been the prevalent immorality, or pornography, or incest, or child abuse, or homosexuality, and on and on; but it hasn't been, not yet at least.

But abortion could finally be the evil horrendous enough, and the threat great enough to the life of all of us, that it rouses us finally to spiritual and political action—our "Pearl Harbor" to enter the war!

Abortion could now be the issue that reveals the absolute moral and spiritual bankruptcy of the prominent philosophies in our God-denying culture—call them humanism, materialism, secularism, liberal religion or whatever.

Abortion could be the issue that rips away the pious facade of these godless philosophies and reveals how murderous they really are. Humanism, for instance, as the essence of hypocrisy, appears to embrace the ethic of Christianity but denies the God who gave the ethic. It makes man god. And, in the name of humaneness and compassion, it reasons it is right to shed innocent blood. When we hold up a picture of an aborted baby, or try to counsel a woman who is grappling with guilt over an abortion, we can say, "This is the fruit of our tragic, idolatrous philosophies!"

But will we become a crying people for crying sins? John Whitehead, in an article, "Christians in the Secular Society,"[2] said:

The question is, How will the majority of Christians respond? One can look the other way *as thousands of unborn children are killed every day*. One can retreat into his safe and comfortable world of Sunday services and fellowship dinners. One can nobly pardon his passiveness by claiming that "out of love" he does not want to offend anyone. But the one who accommodates the world's standards instead of exposing them to the light of biblical truth is no longer following Christ in the true sense.

For the Christian, the bottom line is not what is safe, or comfortable, or inoffensive, but what is true. Christians are to light the world and to salt the earth, and that involves moral confrontation. Though our pluralistic society seeks to eliminate effective Christian influence, we must be faithful to secure a truly open marketplace of ideas.

Whitehead also said:

> If Christians—by personal apathy or external pressures—allow the truth to be muffled, our nation will continue to flounder in a destructive whirlpool of relative values and conflicting laws. Christians will be largely responsible for a culture that breeds crime and immorality, cheapens the value of families, and unashamedly destroys "inferior" human life.[3]

Jeremiah—often called "the weeping prophet"—spoke words that we should proclaim to our nation and our world today.

This is what the Lord says: Do what is just and right. Rescue from the hand of his oppressor the one who has been robbed. Do no wrong or violence to the alien, the fatherless or the widow, and do not shed innocent blood in this place. . . . But your eyes and your heart are set only on dishonest gain, on shedding innocent blood and on oppression and extortion (Jer. 22:3, 17 NIV).

Jesus our Lord was moved deeply when He looked out over His murderous generation (Matt. 23) and pronounce those seven "woes" on it. Those woes unmasked th surrounding culture from behind its pious, pharisaic front. His final words were pointed:

And you say, "If we had lived in the days of our forefathers, we would not have taken part with them in shedding the blood of the prophets." So you testify against yourselves that you are the descendants of those who murdered the prophets. Fill up, then, the measure of the sin of your forefathers!

You snakes! You brood of vipers! How will you escape being condemned to hell? . . . And so upon you will come all the righteous blood that has been shed on earth, from the blood of righteous Abel to the blood of Zechariah son of Berakiah, whom you murdered between the temple and the altar.

I tell you the truth, all this will come upon this generation.

Jesus revealed His tremendous compassion by cryin "Oh Jerusalem, Jerusalem, you who kill the prophe and stone those sent to you, how often I have longed to gather your children together, as a hen gathers her chicks under her wings, but you were not willing" (Matt. 23:37 NIV).

But of course the question is, Will we stand in the gap before God for our culture? Will we speak into the ear of our world both the Word of God and the compassion of God? Will we work to change laws that give official sanction to the shedding of innocent blood? Will we follow the biblical command to "speak up for those who cannot speak for themselves"? (Prov. 31:8 NIV). Will we become mighty in prayer?

Will we?

If we do, the prospect for a mighty spiritual awakening is tremendous for our day. That oft-quoted promise in 2 Chronicles 7:14 is especially appropriate. It speaks of the crying people: "If my people, which are called by my name, shall humble themselves, and pray, and seek my face, and turn from their wicked ways; then will I hear from heaven, and will forgive their sin, and will heal their land" (KJV).

A crying people will not just curse the darkness, but they will light a candle: "Arise, shine, for your light has come, and the glory of the Lord rises upon you. See, darkness covers the earth and thick darkness is over the peoples, but the Lord rises upon you and His glory appears over you" (Isa. 60:1-2 NIV).

God has a dream for us. He has made us in His image and has given us the powerful gift of the capacity to procreate life by an act of will in cooperation with Him. But the twin sins of immorality and murder continue to attack this beautiful gift. Our culture of murder today, filled with idolatrous, humanistic reasonings such as pro-choice, viability of a fetus, and alleged right of a woman to her own body, sanctions the shedding of innocent blood. Who is to blame? We all are!

Will we become personally involved for change? Will intercession, repentance and public involvement become priorities of church, parish and synagogue?

Will we take seriously the warnings—and the promises of the Scriptures?

Or will we continue on in our humanistic, self-seeking pursuits, oblivious to the judgment we could be racing toward—ignoring the cries of the unborn innocents that the Father hears.

Our Lord warned us that the last days would be like the days of Noah: "Now the earth was corrupt in God's sight and was full of violence. . . . So God said to Noah, 'I am going to put an end to all people, for the earth is filled with violence' " (Gen. 6:11, 13 NIV).

Could Isaiah's words (59:7) describe us: "Their feet rush into sin; they are swift to shed innocent blood"? And this: "See how the faithful city has become a harlot! She was once full of justice; righteousness used to dwell in her— but now murderers!" (1:21 NIV).

Isaiah also says: "See, the Lord is coming out of His dwelling to punish the people of the earth for their sins. The earth will disclose the blood shed upon her; she will conceal her slain no longer" (26:21 NIV).

Certainly the judgment upon Babylon in the end times prominently includes her sin of bloodshed. Babylon symbolizes our world system set against God:

> Fallen! Fallen is Babylon the Great! . . . for her sins are piled up to heaven, and God has remembered her crimes. . . . In her was found the blood of prophets and of the saints, and of all who have been killed on the earth (Rev. 18:2, 5, 24 NIV).

"What hope is there, then, for the West?" Alexander Solzhenitsyn has asked.

"The time when the West could save itself by its own exertions may already have passed. To save itself would require a complete change in its attitudes, when in fact these attitudes are still going the wrong way. Instead of girding itself for struggle, the West is still hoping for outside forces to save it, through some kind of miracle . . . but the only miracle that the people of the West can pray for *is a profound change in their own hearts!*"[4]

In the face of our grievous, culminating sin of shedding innocent blood, we must cry out to the Father for a change of heart—and law.

There is, supremely, ultimately no other question before us! Not economic. Not political. Not nuclear.

Hosea knew the question—and the heart of the Father—and could not lay down his pen until he had begged his people to change course—to have a change of heart. His final chapter is a chapter of anguish, yet a powerful passage that beams with the rainbow of hope.

It is just the appropriate Word for America and our world—and most especially you and I—today:

> Return, O Israel, to the Lord your God.
> Your sins have been your downfall!
> Take words with you
> and return to the Lord.
> Say to him:
> Forgive all our sins
> and receive us graciously,
> that we may offer the fruit of our lips.
> Assyria cannot save us;
> we will not mount war-horses.
> We will never again say "Our gods"

to what our own hands have made,
for in you the fatherless find compassion."

The Father responds:

"I will heal their waywardness
and love them freely,
for my anger has turned away from them.
I will be like the dew to Israel;
he will blossom like a lily.
Like a cedar of Lebanon
he will send down his roots;
his young shoots will grow.
His splendor will be like an olive tree,
his fragrance like a cedar of Lebanon.
Men will dwell again in his shade.
He will flourish like the grain.
He will blossom like a vine,
and his fame will be like the wine from Lebanon.
O Ephraim, what more have I to do with idols?
I will answer him and care for him
I am like a green pine tree;
your fruitfulness comes from me."

And finally, Hosea comes to rest:

Who is wise? He will realize these things.
Who is discerning? He will understand them.
The ways of the Lord are right;
the righteous walk in them,
but the rebellious stumble in them.

Notes for Chapter Thirteen

[1] *They Preached Liberty*, Coral Ridge Ministries, p. 127.

[2] *Fundamentalist Journal*, Nov. 1984, p. 21.

[3] Ibid., p. 20.

[4] Franky Schaeffer, *Bad News for Modern Man*, Crossway Books, p. 147.

BIBLIOGRAPHY

Anderson, F.I., & Freedman, David N. *Hosea*, Doubleday,
New York, 1980.

Jackson, Jeremy, *No Other Foundation*, Crossway Books,
Westchester, IL, 1980.

Koop, Everett, & Schaeffer, Francis, *Whatever Happened
to the Human Race?*, Fleming H. Revell, Old
Tappan, NJ 1979.

Powell, John, SJ, *Abortion: The Silent Holocaust*, Argus
Communications, Allen, TX, 1981.

Schlossberg, Herbert, *Idols for Destruction*, Thomas
Nelson, Nashville, TN, 1983.

Cry of the Innocents
Videotape

A videotape presenting the *Cry of the Innocents* message is available through John O. Anderson.

John O. Anderson also travels to speak on the subject of this book.

For information on the videotape or on John O. Anderson presenting his message in person, please write to:

John O. Anderson
P.O. Box 152
Klamath Falls, OR 97601